A Kansas Sunrise

Captured by seven women

by Earlice Switzer-Rupp

"Profound and ageless...a collective narrative of kinship, life and a celebration of memories."

Cover Photograph by Teresa Switzer

Dorrance Publishing Co
585 Alpha Drive
Pittsburgh, PA 15238
Visit our website at *www.dorrancebookstore.com*

ISBN: 978-1-6393-7162-4
eISBN: 978-1-6393-7973-6

A Kansas Sunrise
Captured by seven women
Earlice Switzer-Rupp
'Profound and ageless... a collective narrative of kinship, love & a celebration of memories.'

Table of Contents

Acknowledgement

"Spiritual and Sensitive" are words that come to mind after I read the prose from each of the women that shared a Kansas Sunrise from a warm summer morning. It has been a privilege to surround it with what I thought was just my sorrow, my experience. It was vital once I learned that it was an emotional common narrative that we shouldered together one moment in time. With much appreciation we thank each other for enriching the remaining days to come. Now I speak to you, Angela, thanks for sharing your "power spot" with us. Your experience and the heartfelt awareness born from it are gifts that will always be cherished. To the memory of every strong-spirited descendant of the only remaining all black town west of the Mississippi River, Nicodemus, on the High Plains of Northwestern Kansas.

Prologue

On the third ring, a standard answering recording with a male's voice gave instructions to leave a message.

"Hello, my name is Leesa Rupp." She steadied her voice. "I was calling to speak to Cindy Younger. If this is her, please give me a call back as soon as possible. This is my cell number that you can make the return call to. If this is a wrong number please ignore this message, thank you." Immediately, after closing her cell, Leesa continued to throw whatever she thought might be needed into the open suitcase positioned on a cushioned bench at the foot of her bed. She quickly examined the room to make sure that it was as tidy as possible and made her way into the rest of her house to do the same. After tossing the overnight travel case on the back seat of her car, she backed out of the garage. Her cell phone rang. The voice on the other end sounded cheerful and inquiring.

"Hey stranger! What a surprise, how are you?" Leesa was relieved that it was her old college friend on the other end. She was hopeful that she would receive a call back, in spite of a five-year gap of any form of communication!

"Cindy!" She had to steady her voice once again and fight away tears. "The Old Man is being life-flighted to Wichita in the next hour! Can you be there to meet the helicopter?" She didn't wait for a response. "You need to be his daughter until I can get there." Her polite telephone voice was gone.

"Where is BeBe?" My mother was Cindy's first concern; she loved my parents as her own. Ivalee is my mother's birth name, Bebe was a nickname I gave her when I was twelve. It was a perfect match, in my adolescent mind, to my Daddy's nickname: 'Boo.' "Will your sister, Norma, be there? And when are you leaving?" Leesa responded to each of Cindy's questions in the order they were given.

"Bertha Carter is driving mom to the hospital, which should be about a three-hour drive. And Norma is already in route. I should be there in about eight hours if I don't make my usual stops. The boys are making flight arrangements."

"Okay, I will see you at the hospital. Please just be careful, that's a ten-hour drive, maybe nine, in front of you. I'll call you once he arrives. Love you."

"Love you as well…this means the world to me…thanks so much Cindy."

When the ER doctors were prepared to give a diagnostic review of our dad's condition three days later, the attending physician informed all of us there was nothing they felt would bring him out of the comatose state. A professional and cordial hospital administrator stood beside the Attending physician to give us further instructions. After a quick review of the folder in hand, the doctor addressed the guest waiting room in general. He was sure to keep consistent eye contact toward the most familiar faces - my mother, sister and me.

"We have prepared a room down the corridor to discuss Mr. Freddie Switzer's medical outcome and want to assure you we have done everything to make him comfortable." The administrator's facial expression appeared anxious. Clearly, talking with family was obviously part of her job she disliked. When the doctor finished his explanations, out of the immediate family Leesa, being the initial contact, was the first to speak.

"I've seen that room." Then I turned and gestured to everyone in the waiting room. My two oldest brothers, Louis and Thomas, sat on either side of my mom. My sister was with my youngest brother, Phillip. The room was quiet, I continued, "...it won't be big enough. All thirty-eight people in this room, not including a few close family friends, are here right now because they want to hear some positive news!" I managed to keep my tears in check. My younger brother, Marvin and I were always the most likely to take charge, he put his arm around my shoulder and continued. After he introduced the doctors to every single person, our father's siblings, nephews, nieces, and a few grandchildren, the look on the doctor's face concurred with the words he directed to the woman by his side:

"Well, Penny, it appears that we have a very special patient in our care, so we need to get back to work!" He thanked us collectively, after learning that our dad was the oldest living person in our immediate family along with some additional family history. A few minutes later the two disappeared down the corridor and back toward the ICU. The team of five doctors, specialists in their areas of medicine, were successful but all efforts were short-lived. Two and a half years later a conference room wasn't necessary once again nor was there a consultation with the doctors…

"BEFORE THE SUNRISE"

At exactly 6:00 A.M., all the plans and instructions were being typed into my computer. Several brief phone calls were necessary and agreed upon to honor the simple requests. Each phone call was followed by sincere condolences offered and received. My sister, Norma, was hands-on and managed the rest of the details. These arrangements, after six straight hours, were to be steadfast and were focused on completing the task at hand until they were done. It was my desire to be effective and precise. Years and months before, I had developed no tolerance for debate. After endless hours of doctors, of sterile hallways, of emergency hospital waiting rooms, where our dad had been life-flighted, I operated on automatic pilot that day since I was the one to make the majority of the final decisions. And now, not even from my siblings, there were no objections. It was my responsibility without question, without provocation, to complete and deliver all the documents and obituary outline to the mortuary. Then share everything with my silblings. Just one tap of a finger would end the six hours it took to empty the pain from my heart. To honor our dad, the one person beside our mother, was always steadfast in our lives. Secretly, I believed that he always had a soft spot in his heart for just me. I suppose like most little girls their daddy's are bigger than life. I never had any reasons to fear him.

After examining the documents one more time, every single word brought me closer and closer to the breaking point that I had fought in considerable anticipation. I would have to let go, say goodbye to the one person that loved me all of my life unconditionally. This is something I wasn't always privy to realize. Oftentimes, over the years, I wondered why he would, without a lecture, come to my rescue. Now my protector's journey was finished. The gift that he gave me was his intuitive insight, fearless pride, and a kind and caring mindset towards other people in general.

The night before, after the unwanted phone call, I crawled into my empty bed after a ten-hour shift stocking and sorting greeting cards about happiness, birthdays, anniversaries, and silly little cards of congratulations and achievements. The cards tied to expressions of sorrow and sympathy were the last of the Hallmark cards that needed to be stocked before the store closed at midnight. Prior to this solo task and part-time job, my normal eight-hour, five-day work week was arduous. Steady data entry on a million-dollar project and the inquiries from my work mates alerted me to the fact that I wasn't my normal self. I felt lost within my nagging fears and anxious thoughts. The intuitive gift my dad gave me didn't always include a sense of doom. Instinctively however, this time I could sense that something was happening to someone in my immediate life, and it caused me to lose my balance of being cordial, friendly, and at ease. I just wanted to be in a complete state of mental silence. In reality, which was ironic also, I was in need of comfort. Yet I searched for solitude.

It was a normal Wednesday with the normal deadlines to meet and then the rush to beat midweek traffic to avoid the freeway parking lot of every vehicle known to man trying to reach home. Life, as it were, had become automatic with the need to fill every waking hour avoiding the blindsiding events of the past two years. Everything that had happened was similar to an unexpected and crippling car crash. The eventuality was inevitable that my mental state and now sole existence left me numb. I couldn't help but think about my sister and now my mom. They too had expressed feelings of going through the motions of just living each day as they came, at different times. In my sister's case, a month after our father was hospitalized, her husband had died, six months later her oldest son. For me it was a mutual decision to separate from my marriage which ended in divoice a year later. Now, it was my mother that had lost her mate after sixty-four years. In a matter of three years, these events, one after another, had brought me to a breaking point mentally. It was necessary for me to ignore my emotional scars and concentrate on what I hoped was a well planned schedule of activities. In this way, it would not leave any empty hours to think out loud about anything, particularly thoughts concerning the desires of missing my father's love or the love and attention of a romantic partner. The best possible thought was no thought. To remain blank in my desires until the time came to drown myself in the unexpected but accepted status of emotional abandonment. Oddly though, in my heart, I did not feel that kind of loss. Just emptiness.

It was this incapacitating mindset that prevented me from being in touch with my spiritual connection. The family and emotional ties were channeled into my everyday life. The lesson I was taught as a child within my family home was learning to stay connected and aware of any unannounced predators lurking around the corners. This left me guarded. Such past negative experiences were archived in the recesses of my mind, from which I was generally sheltered. However, there was an exception. Most confusing were those images from my past that visited without warning...in the wee morning hours at that deepest point of sleep. It was an unprotected slumber, free-falling into a "black hole." After twenty-five years, this time the escape from the black hole was different. There wasn't a voice that would whisper gently close to my tear-stained face. It was the voice that would always break the fall, to stop the haunting dreams, causing them to vanish, had itself vanished.

"Leesa, open your eyes. Leesa?" The familiar voice would repeat my name several times to stop my uncomfortable struggle. Afterwards, gentle hands would pull me into secure arms. Instantly my eyes would open and then close all in the same action as I collapsed exhausted against my husband's shoulder. He never asked me about what he called "dreams," but were actually dark and invisible nightmares. Mentally they were mind crippling and seemingly imaginary nightmares! The following and uncounted mornings, over the usual cups of black coffee, I wondered if I talked throughout them once they started.

If memory serves me correctly, only once I had asked, "What do I say? Do I mention names when I dream?"

His answer was simple.

"No, you sometimes wave your hands into the air. You cry a lot." His response sounded troubled, yet given to the morning newspaper from which he didn't take his attention away from. Each time I would think, "*If only I could open my eyes to see the faces!*" If there were faces to see...

I finally gave up trying to remember the details the next morning. So in short order after my dad's death, when the nightmare returned, this time before the nightmare ritual ended, I forced myself awake! Without hesitation I threw the summer blankets away from my body and rushed from the bed to steady myself against my dresser. Immediately I carefully moved the short distance into the bathroom. I stood in front of the vanity sink and mirror splashing cold water on my face. For the first time, there were shadows and distinguishable figures and faces in the mirror with me that floated away into the early dawn of morning. My first anxious thoughts were to call Cindy. My dearest friend and college classmate. She was like a sister that I didn't want to burden, but both of us were in need of comfort. If not her, I wanted to call Angela. Both were women that held my fears and much of my personal history. Angela Bates was the trusted confidant and cousin who had already been entrusted with the unexplained dreams and knew some of the names from the dreams with the exception of one. I didn't even know the name of the young female image. Perhaps later, there would be more time, to explore the tale and unexplained nightmares and dreams but not now. Because of the time and hectic schedule of the day I faced, such a conversation with myself would have to wait. I hesitated and changed my thoughts to prepare for my solo trip. The reality of my discoveries would without doubt accompany me, back home to my family homestead. Suddenly I felt exhausted and vulnerable. Such feelings seemed to happen more times than not since my daddy died. I could feel nothing under each step I took. I was floating in a conscious state of foreboding fear and isolation. Exposed and unprotected after fifty-five years.

In less than a week, I had returned to my hometown along with my siblings to bury our father and the man that I knew with all my heart adored me from the very day he laid eyes on me. I was his fourth child; I benefited from having a father with experience. My two older brothers were typical boys excited to have a baby sister and another member of the family. Under his instructions they readily accepted the responsibility to take care of me in our dad's absence. He was forced to travel away from home often to find steady employment. It was an indicator of that time period and of life. I was also his second daughter. A mixed blessing, I learned later, for my sister. It was joy laced with resentment and sibling jealousy. I was cuddled as a baby with nothing to do but observe everyone else that took care of me for just about every need of a toddler. I was often informed of their waiting on me "hand and foot" with fond laughter when such family stories were told. It was time that revealed such reactions from my sister that were tinted with discontent. Between the two of us, we were born to one father but were raised by two vastly different dads! As the oldest child, her relationship with him was seven years older than my own. I quickly came to see that time changes people, but sometimes people cannot change, or choose not to change. That my sister may not like me became a growing confusion. I kept my distance and denied my heart such unwanted knowledge in my later years. This reaction was the best road to take, because later as adults, she became my best friend, maybe my hero. In short order in our everyday life as girl children I would escape my sister's lack of concern for me and the house work I was assigned to do by becoming the town's best known "tomboy." This was the only alternative growing up surrounded by boys.

Now as adults, when we would return home, for any number of reasons all in all such things would take a back seat. This was the case now as will. It was now a time to acknowledge and offer condolences and comfort to other relatives. Unpredicted loss had become a far too often state of sorrow in our small home town. Like me and my siblings now and the loss of a parent in death was commonplace. (Such was the case less than a month before our dad's death when the Brogden children lost their mother, Billie.) Thinking back over the past decades and countless years of all those that had fallen asleep in death was still emotionally painful. This pain was reflected in the faces of the families left behind. The void left many without words. We were all each other's loved ones, family members and immediate relatives brokenhearted because of the vacancies. These losses left us all with the acute awareness that our hometown was a dwindling hometown.

One such death that left me in a profound state of mourning was from my mother's side of the family. Her name was Clare Clark. She had married my mother's first cousin. She was not just a lifelong relative but a friend to my mom. I remember as a child, the two of them talking for hours on the phone once both homes were settled and children supposedly tucked into bed. During waking hours between the two mothers, sixteen children giggled and talked in whispering tones about their own daily activities, including how to maneuver and plot a way to keep secrets from their parents. It did not matter much; each of these young mothers most likely already knew about such mischievous behavior. In each family, there was always at least one child that enjoyed keeping their childhood secrets "with their momma." During their time spent together both women simultaously acknowledged and ignored the stories that the children told on themselves. They just wanted to savor the small window of time to catch-up on "grown folk talk" or to "ooh and aah" over their favorite soaps. There were times even my inquisitive sister was not sure who Mamma was making noise with on the phone after being shunned and shooed away from being nosey. The only telephone system in the late fifties and early sixties was called a party line for more reasons than being able to chat with four or five people at a time. It was a free-for-all of treasured moments shared whether it was old or new gossip or where heartbreaking news was delivered in quiet tones. The news about Ms. Clara, or "Mama Clara," was one of those times when phones were held onto for dear life and disbelief. It was a painful time, especially for me because of all the many miles that separated me from her "going home" services. Clara was everyone's mom; she was a touchstone and go-to-friend guaranteed. When something needed to be done, if she had not already volunteered, it just was natural to ask Ms. Clara. She was always willing to help do anything. Her "home-going services" mimicked that of a dignitary farewell judging from the number in attendance from the area towns and the visible heartbreak shown for all her children. The endless number of cars stretched for the entire two miles to the local cemetery giving evidence that so many would hold the burden of Clara's absence in their hearts for a very long time.

The same was true regarding heartbreak and absence just a month before my dad's passing, when Billie Brogden, fell asleep in death. She was one of his lifelong childhood friends and cousins. By profession she was a nurse and in life she was a caregiver, wife, and mother. She was always a reserved, quiet and shy woman. Her passing was immediate, and extended my sorrow. The first encounter I shared with her oldest child after his mother and my father had passed was gentle. It was such a solemn void, even when we embraced one another, it was empty; we both had lost our sense of emotions. We had become small children without words, it was only silence and unspoken sorrow. A tender and gentle embrace was all that was adequate and yet necessary to share, to shelter our pain. It was one more unspoken understanding.

These two women, like my mom and a few others, were cornerstones of our lives and the town. They stabilized and built our hometown and mentored our families. The women of Nicodemus that guided me were amazing, insightful, strong, protective, no nonsense tattered pieces of a warm patched quilt that held many secrets and stories in its design. Even in death, their love provided a safe haven of assurance.

More times than not, it was difficult to travel back into the decades of life and now cherished years. There were far too many members in one lifetime that had already left behind so many others to mourn. Ones that I did not get to say farewell to because of distance and time, left me with unexpected and always unwelcome grief. Therefore this Homecoming would be one filled with apologies because of the distance and time that created my absence. Like others however, Homecomings in the past, this would be one to offer continued comfort to our most loved and treasured childhood family members and mentors. Not all expressions of acknowledgement were enough, sometimes there simply were no words. We would share a tender, heartfelt embrace and search the other's, crushed souls with tear-filled eyes. It was a time in life that as closely connected historic and valued families, we were quickly becoming a generation of "orphans." There were those of us that lived in apprehension of such a title. Time had become valued and desired; on the other hand, time had ravaged the soul and left broken hearts and an underlying sense of intimidating anxiety.

Those were the exact words: "How we were becoming orphans" I shared with Angela after she appeared at my mother's doorstep shortly after my arrival to Nicodemus (most times called 'Demus' by the locals). She had come to embrace me in my sorrow and I her's from a different kind of emotional death. Hers was from a unique type of loss and perspective. It was a loss created from a lack of insight into the relationship with her mom and the time lost to unspoken words and buried in secrets.

We both understood I would not join her on a quick little trip here or there to see some of the changes around town. Such things would have to wait for another day. I needed to stay close to my mom to provide her comfort and attention, especially my love. A white picnic table in the yard that was positioned under a little cluster of trees out of July's piercing sun created a cool and private space where we could talk. This was where our separate sorrows of losing a parent melted into one between kindred spirits. .

Before she left, after two profound hours of openly sharing a heart-to-heart, exposing hidden truths, she suddenly declared, "Leesa, come with me, 'monster face!' Monster face was a nickname she gave me years before. Her tear-filled eyes danced with hope while searching mine, willing me to say yes.

"Come with me to my 'Power Spot," she pleaded. I could see clearly that it was a plea from her heart.

I gently wiped tears that slipped from her exhausted eyes down her round soft cheeks and answered, "I will."

"IN THE BEGINNING"

Going to the power spot was given birth due to Angela's tireless efforts to preserve the legacy of the ancestors that had established the little town that was set completely on the south side of highway 24 in Northwestern Kansas called Nicodemus. It was unique and held the distinct honor of producing famous and honorable men and women. There was a great deal of pride in being known as a resident, past and present, of the small all-black town west of the Mississippi River. It was because of its size and rich history that Angela was determined to establish her birthplace a national landmark, my Uncle, Veryl Switzer, also encouraged this distination. And later as a national historic park site that would be governed by descendants with hopes of increasing it's longevity, so that it would not disappear from the maps of Kansas and the United States.

Often, over countless years, Angela received some form of communication from different areas of the United States. These communications were a reminder that she could be proud of the productive history of a historic family town of over eight generations of freed people. At one time those who established the town were considered only as slaves, not men and women. Her primary goal was to convince as many of her relatives as possible to have the same desires she did. However, this was only one of the things that kept her motivated. She wanted as many of her peers to return home and assist in the rebuilding of their home. Until that happened, time and time again, she was rewarded with knowing, eventually that many of her peer group and generation had the same desire by being supportive from a distance., but were tied to life in the city that dictated their personal lifestyles. The cost and way of life that they had become accustomed to needed time before they could be severed to return to Nicodemus, if at all. Therefore, she was aware, mindful and reminded often of the desires of their hearts, they would make that journey back home someday. It was a shared hope that they would come back home as she had done. Meanwhile, they would return home for family events and realize that their home base was dwindling and being neglected. She hoped with each visit they could sense the urgency or the need to take action before the possibility of losing what remained of a never again rich history in time she had fought for. Maybe the support could conquer the ravages of that same dubious time.

Continually, Angela tried to explain why it was so important to join forces with her. She taught by example to the potential and future settlers, that it was a privilege and honor to still live in such a town with its rich history of struggle and achievement. It was from this attitude that she had gained the position as the preserver of history for our hometown of Nicodemus, Kansas. This title was bestowed by a handful of orginal cousins that took part in establising an organization that joined together, for the survival of Nicodemus. The group decided that the name of Nicodemus Historical Society (NHS) would include anyone that wanted to become a member. The little group of five; Angela Bates, Earlice, i.e. "Leesa" & Phillip Switzer, Twillia Moore and Vickie Sayers, was organized with the purpose of maintaining and recovering the title of the only all "black town" west of the Mississippi River. Coupled with her drive and profession as a teacher, Angela wanted to teach the generations coming after her the lessons about achievement and struggle through the history of their own family heritage as a people of freed slaves. The heritage of people documented and established in the early spring of 1877 was connected by one word. Family.

Without a doubt the determination and steadfast deligence to keep Nicodemus on a paper map and any other form of technology, was a constant desire that would exist for over thirty years. Keeping her hope focused and alive was necessary. It was re-enforced from receiving communication and requesting any monetary plagues that would be supportive from different places in the United States. Within those years she unearthed historical artifacts from legal records on file at the local library and county seat. Many insights come naturally from the three black cemeteries. They provided many connections todate where the majority of the historic heritage still exists. Etched on tombstones by the departing dates of their deaths, a common expression declared, "they're with the Lord now." Then and now words of bittersweet sorrow, passed down generation after generation as a reminder that nothing is permanent.

It was in the same fashion of discovery and research that weaved such information together that Angela found this once treasured and special place from her past. She later called it the "Power Spot." It was a forgotten discovery from her childhood years ago. Instantly, this awareness fortified all of her reasons to continue to promote her deep-rooted desires. Her motto going forward was "the master has already written the script," and instantaneously she was certain that God's hands had directed her every step back to her past as a young girl. Even without a solid idea of how it would eventually come together, she knew this new found place would be a powerful piece in rewarding her struggle and a discovery that would also strengthen her own personal hopes of healing.

This place of power was a destination that Angela wanted to share with other women no different than herself, a descendant of Nicodemus. In fact it could be that for any guest or family friend in search of spiritual healing. Anyone, from different parts of the country, would also and always be welcomed. Therefore, she was certain that going to the power spot would be the perfect stimulation to the women in the various families. After all it was a place where she found her reality and continued direction with purpose. This new found awareness came without warning and pure innocence. She discovered it after a sudden summer rainfall and a brilliant double rainbow.

Immediately once it dawned on her how familiar the surroundings were, Angela took a few more photos of the headstones with etchings of faded names and dates where she stood, located in the middle of the Samuel Cemetery. She made a 360 degree surveillance twice where she stood. At that precise moment it was clear what she needed to do. The essence of the location and memory had to be shared with the other women. It was a place she would come to treasure for the rest of her life. In her heart it was a place where she understood the responsibility of reaching true womanhood and ascertaining the meaning of maturity. With excitement, Angela waded back in the direction of her car, in knee high prairie grass and headed home back to her home in Bogue. Her prayers and hopes had to come true. "Going to the power spot" would create curiosity through word-of-mouth. And that is exactly how this early Saturday morning adventure became an unannounced hoped for tradition.

Like the rest of the hometown celebrations in Nicodemus, this early morning event fluctuated in size and was shared forward from one person to the next who was in search of a life outside of the city rat race. A lifestyle of a peaceful and quiet country living. It would be one more cherished activity especially created for the women. It was a highly anticipated, pre-dawn drive to a hillside location to make personal vows at the beginning of a new day. Some vows were spoken aloud, some silent, protected within the heart. But the most important spiritual request was always to strengthen family connections for continued hometown longevity. In Angela's heart, and over the past twelve years since its conception, she just knew it had become a highlight of the best time of year: The week of the annual Nicodemus Emancipation Homecoming Celebration.

"A FORGOTTEN DISCOVERY"

Angela Bates's Power Spot discovery happened entirely unexpectedly after one of her normal days of exploring the countryside. She was continuously in search of history and any information on deceased ancestors that would help tell the stories of Nicodemus' history. While taking random roads without signs, Angela felt lost and wasn't sure where the road would lead. She continued to drive her little white two door car several more miles down the seemingly seldom driven chalk-colored dirt road as she looked for a good place to turn around. Instantly, she caught her breath. Losing the presence of time and her existence, she adjusted her speed. Slowly she brought the car to a crawl and promptly recognized one of her childhood summer playgrounds. She felt lost in time as she applied the brakes, bringing the car to a complete stop. With a little apprehension, she stepped out of the car after the dust had settled following her arrival.

It was a late morning on a chilly spring day driving on out of the way, country roads heightened Angela's curiosity, especially since the foliage was minimal, she could see more details of her surroundings. Once out of the car, she made a complete circle and surveyed the horizon in one continuous motion until her attention returned to the abandoned buildings brought from the past. Presently, they were void of nature's overgrown foliage of previous years.

Her astonishment was one of praise but simple, "Oh, my God, this is the place, I can't believe it!" Immediately she hopped back into her car. Made two sharp and careful turns and headed to her family's farmhouse, a mile north of Nicodemus, to retrieve her sister Cheryl. The day before with much excitement to be with her family, Cheryl had arrived from California. By the time the pair had returned, the sun was sliding toward the late evening, leaving the surrounding horizon in layers of purple hues and orange mixed with blue highlights of mystic colors. Cheryl, like her younger sister, was completely sold. She exclaimed in awe and whispered to her that they should have brought their mom and how much she loved the early evening of the setting sun.

Before dusk and the sun disappeared, on the way back to the farm, Angela explained every summer vacation and details from the past she could remember to her sister again, just in case she had forgotten, wanting to refresh her memory. Reminding her about how she and their brother Clint and all the other cousins from the immediate area would spend hours upon hours at that very location playing games into the late hours of night. Entertaining and challenging each other on horseback, as well as feeding and attending to the other farm animals as well. Living on a farm wasn't just filled with fun; caring for the livestock was the main source of work, but it was also enjoyable and rewarding. Even though most livestock were raised for food, there were hopes on occasion to win a blue ribbon and profit at area annual county fairs. Other times it was done for community activities and tasks to learn and receive honors as members in the 4-H club. Being associated with such an affiliation was character building. Having qualities that the 4H's repersented, known as Head, Heart, Hands, and Health was a good thing. It labed farms and farmers with a seal of breeding good livestock. Like horses, they were used for both fun, extra help and of course herding cattle. Such possession as a horse was mixed with a little pride of ownership and a noteworthy sense of accomplishment.

Therefore, whenever I personally reminisced about the past, on that very hillside road, where the power spot was discovered, it was impressive to me, as it was for any on-lookers to watch one of the three sisters that lived on the property during the summer with their grandparents, ride a horse, as if experts. Any one of them could champion a horse race; their ability to handle such majestic animals was also fearless. And they always gladly welcomed the chance to win a losing race against Leonard Jones who had little shame in out-racing any girl. He was usually the one to challenge them to a race. His conquest beyond horseback riding, was flirting with girls, in more ways than one. As time progressed having such a reputation held little value to him. Of course his give-a-damn disposition was both ignored and desired by most of the local girls living in town or from the countryside in general. Any flirtatiousness shown to him only heightened his physical desires towards girls who wanted his attention and made it noticeably clear they were willing to win whatever time he would offer in return. This type of behavior added to his mischievous behavior, even if it wasn't needed. So, I found it surprisingly odd that he showed me any interest because I had shown him none. Eventually, he made his presence known, all of a sudden, I too was intrigued by his bad-boy disposition, interest and attention that he found me, of all people, pretty. Those were the reasons mixed with my own curiosity and because he was extremely athletic, handsome and persistent, that Leonard was the first boy I had ever kissed.

Reflecting on the past, it took a little less than a decade during and after high school that I finally accepted his words, that I "owned his heart and always would." In the innocence of our youth, it never occurred to either of us that we would eventually be caught in a "*Romeo and Juliet*" scenario. After all, it was assumed by most "in the know" regarding the relationship, that our "puppy love" was just a childish crush. Such things were considered as "adjustments" to becoming adults and supposedly would be short lived. Instead the relationship encumbered us both for our separate lifetimes. Before that and the passing of time during our youth we were both thankful not to be the only ones to wear such a badge of gossip from old and young alike. In fact, even though we had a distant kinship, there were several kissing-cousin relationships during the adolescent years that ended after our school years.

But all in all, prior to following parental guidance to leave home and get a college education, as teenagers we lived in an adventurous community of small country towns and an idyllic lifestyle. Working was just as natural as having fun and rewarding. It helped maneuver all four seasons of the years to come. When it was time for chores, we worked together side-by-side with our parents. They taught us about life and nature. How something as simple as the weather and the effect it could have on people's actions. Such a common sense tool we would need to survive in the big cities of the world as my dad would sternly make his point to all his children. Not to mention how to stay and keep our city relatives out of trouble when they would come to visit us, their "country cousins," as we were fondly called.

During the summer it was the best time to illustrate what it meant to be a "country cousin," and clearly it was a time of freedom. We demonstrated our ability to our parents that we could be reliable. They were adventurous days of discovery and responsibility. There were County fairs, drive-in picture shows, baseball games, and platform dances with a live band to entertain everyone after the harvest and the long hot days in the fields were over. After a full day and the early evening activities were over, the anticipation of sleeping in the vast out-of doors, couldn't come fast enough. Our beds were in the back of wheat trucks atop of packing blankets, laid over the extra grain left in the trucks just for that purpose. To stare into the night under star-filled skies was mesmerizing. We would catch lightning bugs and carefully put them into soda bottles or mason jars and pretend that they were bright enough to play as late as our hearts desired. This kind of nighttime fun was always short-lived by hearing our names called in the distance to come home. Or if our bodies were beyond exhausted and the need for sleep caused us to seek the pathway back home all on our own accord.

During daylight hours, after morning chores or on the weekends, the Solomon River could be found by the well-traveled path that my brothers and our double-cousins, the four Alexander brothers, Gary, Dale, Juan and Robert, used to escape the townsite and play and hunt as often as possible. We lived next door to each other. A large cottonwood tree that we climbed and played in for hours and several rows of flowers, separated the properties. Our ages staggered one another. Twelve was the sum of our two families, an even dozen, counting our parents. When thinking back on the many hours we played together, it was like having eight brothers instead of four. Most times, for no particular reason, it occurred to me that I was always the only girl, although at the time it wasn't even a consideration. I learned quick enough to hold my own and to blend in as best I could to be a part of every adventure the boys embarked upon. Of course there were always the times I had to do girl stuff and wasn't allowed to "follow those boys around." Remembering the sound of my grandma's voice would bring back the most profound feelings and thoughts, with a smile to my face. Other times I was banned from going with my brothers during hunting season, it was when only the "men" went hunting. The four oldest boys of the group were armed with their guns or bow and arrows. All of them were trained and very proud marksmen. My cousin Dale strived to be the best with stiff competition from my brothers. All the boys were born athletes, excelling in any sport in which they participated in, as individuals or as team members. They were known statewide and put the local high school we attended, located in Bogue five miles away, on the map. Because of their abilities, it was automatic that I was in constant training as a tomboy, an athlete in my right. On occasion, I still sensed that I was still just a girl to them. Which made the times that I could tag along special and Juan, number five of the pecking order of boys, made sure to protect me when we went to the river to fish or just play in the cool water until there was just enough sunlight left to dry our clothes by the time we needed to return home just in time for supper.

Other than the bulk of summer days spent at the Solomon River, that snaked a pathway a good solid mile South of Nicodemus, this hilltop south of Bogue called the "Power Spot" was sure to draw some to visit for the first time perhaps. Others, maybe on a Sunday afternoon, would return to reminisce and share memorable adventures that held many childhood secrets. Many could recount the hours spent exploring the sloping valley directly behind the oversized wooden barn shaded with traces of paint of undetermined colors; the heartbeat of most farms. For city folks and travelers, it was the main attraction of farm-life giving way to curiosity and child-like imagination. For many of the other homesteaders, farmers' wives in particular, it had served to have the best pickings of just about any wild blackberries and plums to preserve in small mason jars in the valley. It also contained the meatiest black walnuts any trees could produce. Majority of the uncultivated soil was black and rich beneath a layer of wild silky grass, and stretched for many miles. It was used for pastureland so cattle and horses could graze free from their daily toil of farm work.

Once in a while on quiet Sundays, on an afternoon drive, while sharing memories from the past we would travel to that hillside south of Bogue. As adults during times when we missed the past, the two of us would reminisce about our coming-of-age years. Angela found such pleasure when she would ask me out of the blue for seemingly no particular reason, "Do you remember why I love this place so much?" She would continue, not needing me to respond. "Because it's peaceful. I have always found solace here. It's a power spot. Mine." Her voice was a whisper to express her feelings. The "spot" had become a special place for her. Sometimes her expressive thoughts varied and usually these inquiries were followed with a distant random thought. Sometimes a very personal tidbit was shared about missing her mom. Just as the things we shared with each other were also personal, so of course I understood and knew why. She wanted to remember all the little details that a mother gives to her daughter for the days yet to come in their life.

Immediately, I would say, "Tell me, I love remembering the days when we were young, especially the ones we spent on Sunday afternoons at the Bronson's farm."

"I know you know why the 'power spot' means so much to me…I think about this place all the time...It's so important to me." She would speak in the direction her eyes lead her thoughts, toward the valley's natural floor and sloping landscape. She kept her eyes averted to avoid mine. She did not want me to see or share her sorrow. Then she would continue in an uplifted mood. "That whole experience when we were younger was amazing. It was the first time in my entire life I'd ever seen a full rainbow, and like magic, there was another one, a double rainbow." She declared with such enthusiasm. Then she would pause, as if it were necessary for us to remember that day. I said nothing but continued to be motionless and would listen to her silence. "Don't you remember, Leese? We were riding horses, and it was maybe the first time Clint and I got to come back to Demus by ourselves. We stayed with Aunt Bernice and Uncle Harry that summer."

Of course I did remember, but she needed to tell her story from so long ago it was necessary to mend her heart. After all it was hers to tell, as I quietly listened. It was the day we were invited to her fathers' relatives' family farmhouse three and half miles south of Bogue to ride horses. Neither of us could hardly wait to saddle up and go for a ride. Even a storm brewing in the direction of our destination, was not enough to deter us. Nothing was going to stop us. However, shortly after arriving and exchanging greetings, we all had to take shelter in the barn from the sudden downpour of rain. It ended just as quickly as it came, leaving the air fresh and clean.

Since I did not care for storms, I had to interject at that very moment of her story. "Yep. But do you remember those ugly black clouds and the lightning?" I stated with emphasis.

"The wind scared the daylights out of me, too. I just knew we would see a tornado any minute… The look on your face was hilarious, just like now." Angela's laughter was contagious. Then she continued her story.

"But as soon as the little storm passed and the raindrops were barely following, we got back on the horses and headed towards the pasture, and suddenly there it was. A full rainbow appeared, within seconds there was another one, in tandem, a double rainbow. I was speechless. I remember throwing my arms in the air and weeping like a baby. Something just went through every fiber of my being!" she stated with such exhilaration. I always thought that any moment she was going to perform a reenactment.

"Yes, I do remember that!" I confirmed with exaggeration. Only because she had managed to scare the daylights out of me when she started shouting. It was a wonderful summer day, how could I not remember. "With every single word, you always paint a perfect memory from the past, back into existence! Just like the rainbows from one end of the horizon to the other. The colors were brilliant; it was a perfect moment." I willingly agreed because it was.

"Exactly!" Angela continued with a rush of nostalgia and excitement. "Remember how we could see every single town starting with Zurich's grain elevator, then Palco's, Demar Church steeples, of course Bogue, and most important, Nicodemus!" The account pulled at my heart. It left us both spellbound as we stared in every direction from the top of this hill. It appeared the rainbow was a protective color barrier to guard over each small town that was nestled between the myths told about rainbows. They were all special little towns nestled between each preverbal pot of gold at the end of every rainbow. Even when there wasn't a rainbow during all those times when we came back, it was still serendipitous. So it was confirmed that this place was where energy could be captured into the heart of those in need of comfort.

Misty-eyed Angela continued.

"Seeing that double rainbow that day was a sign. It was the beginning of discovering such wide-open spaces and the desire in my heart that would drive me straight out of California one day and back home, back home to Nicodemus."

"I know, it always surprises me when this place crosses my thoughts, we were only fifteen-years-old, it feels like 1,000 years ago. We were so happy, very innocent, and in love with everything." After one more full circle viewing that day, reluctantly we let the horses we were riding take the lead to find the others on horseback along the trail to the Solomon River.

The Solomon River consisted of 184 miles and played a major part in the fact that Nicodemus was settled in the northern part of the high plains of Kansas. It came from the middle basin of Missouri and snaked its way in ascending and gradual climb between small valleys, across the grass and desolate prairie lands headed westward. Just at the halfway mark of the state, the River diverted into two seperate directions. At the fork in the River a section went further northward and the other remained in a southward flow. For no particular reason that I could venture upon, the Solomon River split, as water determines its own path. However, the smaller groups of Exodusters and freed slaves, who were not able to travel by train, stayed on the southern path and the most abundant part of the river teeming with fish and the main water source they would need for the journey ahead. Like freedom, water was viewed as a lifeline for survival, as it was for the independent and weary groups of people seeking their own freedom.

The earliest settlers that responded to the beckoning call from an advertisement to "freedom" and a guarantee of ownership, were privileged enough to travel by train. Once their destination was reached in the town of Ellis, their journey on foot and wagon would establish the Ellis Trail that would connect them to Nicodemus. They also quickly recognized that the fall season was imminent, so the small group of eager settlers wasted little time once they discovered the final location five miles away, based on several signals of smoke that appeared to come from the ground they longed to call home. Soon, after crossing the Solomon River, in short order, they moved a mile further north and dug into the land for the only available shelter against the approaching cold long winter. Their first homes were made from the ground called "sod" or "dug-outs." There were no other options because of the land's barren state. As were the means to construct any framed buildings of any size, the land was hard and covered with buffalo grass. The one saving and unexpected help came from the neighborly Potawatomi Indians that inhabited the land. A bond of friendship was established that was never recorded in the history books but lived on between the two groups and provided the settlers with hope as a prayerful gift directly from God!

Perhaps for the first time I, too, after those visits to the hillside, had seen the beauty of everyday life I had growing up as being a place like no other because of the stretched-out landscape and the mixtures of valleys and outlines of the other hills that raised to alternating levels of elevations. Once we gathered with the other riders, the position where we sat atop a small hillside on horseback south of the big barn, gave us a privileged view of the valley decorated with large cottonwood trees that snaked throughout our vision, only to disappear and to reappear again and follow the streams of the Solomon River. The flow of the river was sometimes made up of small paths of steady trickling streams of water and were only depicted because of the trees. It did not have a visual point of ending or beginning. Many times reflecting on the past of my own childhood concerning the Solomon River and time spent with my brothers, it never occurred to me that the river had its own history. It was a place where my Grandpa Fred would stand for long periods of time and watch the clear cold-water flow under the wooden bridge beneath him. Usually after all the barrels were filled with water in the truck by his adoring grandchildren. I often wondered if he had lost something in the River and would find it again one day. I carefully tucked such intimate thoughts and feelings back in the nebulous, of my very observant young mind. With older and younger siblings, making me the middle child, I naturally thought it was my responsibility to make sure everyone was happy. Which I wasn't always able to achieve when it came to my grandparents.

Giving my attention back to Angela, I remember watching her and the passion reflected in her eyes and foreboding fixated stare. Clearly this place left her captivated. She could not take her eyes off the memory where the rainbows had appeared. From end to end, the arch of the deep, colorful half-moon rainbows gave us both a deeper sense of appreciation and hope for two young women like us. We may have even had a delusion that the rainbows were just for us that summer day. In the reality of my thoughts and from what my mother shared with me as a child, I knew that the rainbow was a promise from God; it was his signature of hope, it said so in the Bible. Something I would cling to all of my life was the faith of trusting in what the image of the rainbow represented - A guarantee promise from God himself.

The neghing and shaking heads of the horses informed me that it was time to resume the trek of the lower grounds of the picturesque little farm to join with, yet again, the other riders. I watched that day as Angela occasionally wiped away her tears and I wanted to embrace her. But as much as I wanted to, being on horseback dictated that such things would have to come later. That summer was a turning point not just for Angela but also for me as well. I was introduced to my hometown through her eyes. Going forward on that emotional day, neither of us would talk about the end of summer and manipulated every possible excuse and reason to be together. All we wanted to do was live a fairy tale summer that would make a Huck Finn charater envious of our endless imaginations to keep us in trouble in the days that followed.

I repositioned myself in the saddle and felt unexpectedly foreloin, perhaps as Angela appeared to me. In a few weeks she would leave, summer would end. But neither of us could predict that we had one more summer as teenage girls together. For me I was the most excited because I was spending my first summer away from home in California with Angela. We were both beyond the clouds happy when we found out mid-summer. Of course, the actual trip would not take place until after Homecoming, which I was thankful for. There was no way I ever wanted to miss a family or hometown reunion! Plus, this would allow me to share with Angela everything that took place once I reached my destination, since she couldn't be there.

That was the last fun-filled summer we shared together. Graduating into the positions as upperclassmen in High school, along with the challenge of the added responsibilities at home as older children. When I returned home from the west coast, it was easy to discern the vast difference of life generally speaking from concrete and little square fenced-in yards, to the out of doors and endless spacious place in which to play. I was glad to be back home. In short order, the years that followed became a decade. Life switched from adolescence to adulthood and time completely changed perspectives and the burden of the enviable realities of no longer being considered a child. However for both of us, as women, the desires, memories and love for our hometown remained the same. My desires to keep Nicodemus thriving were at a distance since I lived out of state. Even so, I was readily available to assist in any way possible, to work on or advise on any ideas or project to keep Nicodemus in operating condition and moving forward into the future. It was something I felt necessary that I had to do in my life. To return home as often as possible, especially during homecoming for our annual hometown celebration. It was a yearly event anticipated by all the other local communities as well. Such activities provided friends, not only family, to catch up with people that were instrumental in their life from the past also. Besides the usual activities during the harvest season, immediately after the school year was over, July was the best month of the summer. At every opportunity I returned home so it seemed natural that most residents and visiters, expected me to be the onsite, hands-on, and "go to" person for whatever was needed or forgotten. Even my other out-of-state cousins had forgotten that I didn't live in the most precious place in the world to me. It was precious simply because it was where my dad and mom were raised and still lived.

Therefore, over time because I was home so often, settle comments were made regarding the lack of attention I played in the "limelight" along with Angela! Either from Angela's unexpected but casual comments or those of other individuals, I couldn't express personal doubt even if I prayed that it wasn't true. A classmate from high school exposed my own denial at one point in time. The envious comments made from my dearest childhood cousin, my first girlfriend, the verbal jealousy that she displayed were real and couldn't be hidden, not even for five days during Homecoming. The rest of the 360 days out of the year were left to my confused imagination. One such comment as I recalled, was spoken as an afterthought, I had hoped anyway. I had attempted to offer Angela a compliment for a job well done.

"You have outdone yourself! The program you presented was outstanding." Her reply was short and complacent.

"You think so?" I ignored the tone in her voice.

"For sure, couldn't you tell by the applause and the number of people that had questions for the guest speaker and regarding the overall performances? There are alot of people that admire you Angela." Her unexpected reply surprised me.

"Yeah, right. I doubt that. More times than not...everywhere I go to give presentations there is always someone that will ask about you! And how neat it is that I am kin to you!" The look on my face should've been enough, but I replied anyway.

"Really? You're kidding right? Why?"

"You surely must know that. After all you were the best female athlete in the area, besides all the guys thinking that you were so gorgeous!"

Before I could protest, the conversation was interrupted by another attendee during the homecoming activities, with more questions for Angela. Her last word to me, "gorgeous" wasn't offered or perceived as a compliment! The entire encounter, although brief, was intinally hurtful and removed from my thoughts. Why wouldn't people know me, I was born in Kansas and was an area resident for almost twenty-five years after that.

On the other hand, during my absence Angela seized every opportunity to weather the challenges of living on the high plains of northwestern Kansas. As she had promised she became an area resident and settled in nearby Bogue. Her desires and love for Nicodemus were driven. It was something she had to conquer by remaining focued and steadfast whenever possible. Curiously enough, with so much to keep anyone preoccupied in that part of the state, it soon became evident to me that the majority of the things told to me were true. This awareness was based on actions and exclusion due to who I was and my family name; so I was informed. Seldom was I personally included to provide history to reporters and researchers, regarding the "viewpoint of the children" that actually lived and grew up in Nicodemus. This knowledge of missed opportunities overshadowed my concern and damaged feelings. Feelings of rejection were laid to rest because I didn't want to accept them as the truth. If such information were true and factual, it gave me concern with acute awareness that a great deal of valuable history between us was being ignored by her and would go unrecorded. I needed to find a way to remedy the situation because I didn't want to lose our childhood innocence for whatever reason. Even more so, I didn't want the youthful innocence of such historic years, to include information from other individuals, or that of Nicodemus, be buried under the emotional illness of a damaged ego and most likely, an over-exhausted sense of neglect and of pride.

Once I removed the rose colored glasses, it was clear that the most important thing necessary was to maintain a positive disposition. To remain silent and encourage the one thing that kept Angela motivated. To have her name replace mine out of the mouths of the locals and those in neighboring towns. In my mind it was a very small price to consider, especially since it was early in the game of restructuring Nicodemus. The re-building and modification of five deterioating buildings was visible and on the horizon, thanks to Angela's undying determination. Yet again however, during an off-season of no particular activity or event, negative words were confirmed with her own words one day. I wanted to ignore this entire concept. I struggled with so many mixed feelings of belief and disbelief. I even wondered who could be feeding her such hurtful thoughts and for what selfish gain. Each time I could find no conclusions.

But when my dad's casual statement was voiced aloud it was different. I had to take his words more seriously. "Angie is a good kid, but she has a jealous streak when it comes to you, Leese. You just can't see it?" I didn't answer, but I heard his words and always trusted my father's instincts. His words were confirmed by those of her own one day when I returned back home to our hometown for a brief visit. Angela was busy working in her kitchen making barbecue sauce. After our usual greetings, she explained the reason for her task at hand and would be leaving soon. We both agreed that we could catch-up later in the weekend. Then out of the thick aroma of the rich smells of her kitchen, she made a simple statement.

"A couple weeks ago. I ran into one of your old grade school classmates. Of course he asked about you. Everywhere I go, once people find out that I'm from Demus, your name always comes up!" Her tone surprised me, and I chose to ignore it with my light hearted reply.

"Really? Did they give you their name?"

"No. I don't think so, if they did I can't remember what it was. And as usual, people always remind me how great you and all the guys were in sports!" I let my silence end the conversation. Even though her words put clothes on the things shared with me over time, it was still the one thing I had refused to believe when it was brought to my attention.

But, on the other hand, my silence would keep my hometown alive and a place I would always have to call home. My desire was that Angela would be the avenue to accomplish my hope, my prayers. My silence was a small price to pay because in my absence and wisdom, I had learned that the past can't be changed. This knowledge of her feelings would not deter my love, concern, my friendship and kinship that connected us as cousins. The one thing that secured the bridge in our life was our love for our hometown and the two little girls that we once were in our innocence as children. When, once upon a time, true friendships were built on honest and stable foundations of unity and trust.

So again and again, over time, the decades that had passed before our very eyes continued to bring families together for one reason or another. Unfortunately it was not always our hometown celebration or any other seasonal activity. Sometimes, more times than not, time took its toll. It was those times that we gathered to say goodbye to our loved ones because they had fallen asleep in death. This time we had lost a pillar of a middle aged man. A husband and father, Clint Bates. He was Angela's hero and her second oldest brother. Between the two of them, more so for Clint, the desire to leave California and return home, back to Kansas, wasn't a fairy tale. After thirty years of living his dream in Nicodemus, Clint's final home was a marker in the Mount Olive Cemetery located northwest of town. His death came without a warning, as heart attacks usually do. His horse was dressed completely geared as a "Buffalo Soldier" and stood at full attention at the gate of the cemetery, when the wagon that carried his owner rolled past the entrance of his resting place. As all funeral services are, this was profoundly solomn and quiet. Only in the faces and the eyes were there words that explained pain and confusion. The luncheon was a normal place where laughter and chatter and memorable moments could be found, this time it was respectful and again quiet. It was later in the day after the family's farewell from the dining hall, that Cheryl, Clint and Angela's sister, once again wanted her sister to explain to her two daughters the important story about going to the "power sport." It would be their first time to go, to include most of the family as well, to experience this now treasured location that Cheryl could not stop making references about when sharing the history of Nicodemus with her friends.

Because Angela's sorrow was profound, her heart was beyond broken, explaining the power spot was not what she wanted to do. She wanted to take the trip by herself, just be there alone, more than anything to empty her soul into God's care. Therefore her explanation was brief and without her normal enthusiasm and details. Her family understood and recognized that it was beyond Angie's abilities to cheerfully rejoice in the life she lived during the summers as a young country girl. The next visit would be a solo flight. The words Angela held in her mind were locked within her thoughts and wouldn't leave her mouth as words. She remained speechless for hours. The only thing that was most important to her was missing and wanting her brother Clint to be alive. She didn't know exactly how to explain to the others of her pain. The internal pain in her heart would vanish; if only he was still within reach, then she wouldn't feel confused and lost without him. Over and over, when inquired of anything by anyone her reply had no passage to leave her body. She had become mute. Her state of silence was fueled by the loss of the family's oldest member, which also stifled her mental apprehension. She felt emotionally drained and responsible and unable to be in charge of everything that the family always expected her to have accomplished.

Her mother's sister and Angela's aunt Ernestine Van Duvall died one month before her brother. Even though this was expected, it was a two-fold loss for Angela. She was left without a business companion and her best friend in just a few weeks time. It was after the loss of these two family members, both in 2004, two months apart, before the July homecoming celebration, that she placed a silver butterfly bracelet around a "talking stick" that would be used at each gathering at the 'power spot', a gift from her Aunt Ernestine. It was beautiful and symbolic. Like the butterfly, she wanted each woman to have the experience of a transformation and become wiser women. It was poetic. From youth as mere caterpillars, to delicate and beautiful butterflies of maturity and wisdom. This wisdom would be shared in the early morning hours after the sunrise.

All agreed the ritual and routine of visiting the "power spot", the ambiguities of emotions and gradually sharing the energy of the location with others, made it a special place of which to be a part. It was also unique because of the aura they experienced. It was that kind of unexplained pull to this "power spot" that she hoped would provide her comfort for always. For always came the very next year. In August 2005, a month after the homecoming celebration, Angela found herself at the "power spot". It wasn't a normal visit. It was one that was necessary to keep from falling apart. Her struggle to continue to live life was drowning her existence and she felt in her heart, she would lose the battle.

Less than a handful of days after homecoming, as always, the immediate mass departure of families returning to their lives in the cities in various parts of the country was over. And now she felt the burden of loneliness. The death of Charlesetta, Angela's mother, only elevated her empty emotions to a state of mental exhaustion, into a black hole. Charlesletta's departure from this earth came a month later to end the summer months and after another year of the homecoming celebration. It was an untimely month and time of the year for so many friends and family members. The beginning of another school year was under way and all vacation time was depleted. As it were, anytime would never be acceptable when death separates and leaves the living abandoned. It would be difficult to have the majority of her family and friends, who had recently left to return back to their homes, come back for the funeral. Therefore the ceremony was small and quiet, which was completely opposite of the woman her mother was. Charlesletta Williams-Bates knew how to draw attention to her cheerful and elegant presence. She loved hats and being seen without one was not natural. She was diligent about wearing the most beautiful hats to complement her very stylish and colorful outfits. This made it odd that her passing was quick and quiet when life departed from her fragile body. It was after her mom's death that Angela lost her direction, once again so soon, before she was able to heal from the previous year. This time going to the power spot as usual wouldn't be a shared experience. The drive would be a solo destination where she could receive consolation and peace in honest, unspoken conversations with herself from a higher spiritual power - our heavenly father and creator!

When she arrived, there was a red truck parked on the side of the road, not far from where she so desperately wanted and needed to be. She was in search of understanding and forgiveness spoken aloud from the heart in outcries of painful declaration. In search of ending her sorrow only God and her mother could provide, even after her final exit from this earth. Before the tears came accompanied with an image of her mother's inquiring eyes, she paused and delayed the moment to speak her heart's truth into the void of space; there was an instant peace that surrounded her. The lingering words in her thoughts fell dormant. She stood peaceful and still with her endless days of sadness at her side.

"I love this place." The man's voice was deep but soft. He apparently was the owner of the red truck. He seemed to have appeared out of nowhere. "Why are you here?" It was a simple, noninvasive and curious question.

"I love this spot, too. Actually I love this whole area. I call it my 'power spot,' Angela whispered.

"That's exactly what this place is, a power spot." The apparent awareness was a clairvoyant statement made to the endless view that stretched into an endless afternoon horizon.

On cue, from the sloping hills, suddenly a Red Tail Hawk out of nowhere flew a short distance in front of the two motionless figures. Skillfully the Red Tail Hawk, soaring higher and then sinking, disappeared into a grove of nearby trees.

"Wow!" Angela exclaimed. "Did you see that?" she asked the man with no name. Keeping her eyes fixed on the top of a line of trees with hopes of the hawk reappearing, she waited, avoiding eye contact with this complete stranger.

"I train birds of prey." The man's voice remained gentle, soft, and deep.

"I always wanted one of those kinds of birds, a falcon to be exact." She continued to look out for the hawk. "Birds are fascinating."

"That's why I like that particular raptor. They are very fascinating birds to train." There was no reply to the man's words; she had become lost in time and thought. Finally she turned to gain additional information from the stranger, but just like the Red Tail Hawk, the man was gone as if he just disappeared. At first, she found it a little disconcerting, but gradually she became completely and emotionally absorbed, once again, in profound thought regarding her mom. She was alone as she had hoped, no longer concerned about the man as she stood alone.

"I do love birds, all kinds of them. So did my mom." Her words were whispered only to the horizon. With great determination, she fought against the tears that blurred her view. She was not ready to consume the pain and deep sorrow they would bring. Within a few minutes, she felt the urge to leave. At that precise moment, the thought occurred to her that the missing man could have been an angel because he had simply disappeared. As she looked around in no particular direction, she crossed the vacant road back to her car. Once she reached her car, she looked up and then down the road in both directions - nothing. After climbing into the car, she pondered on the man in the red truck long enough to experience a sense of calmness. A gentle breeze flowed into the open windows as she started the car. Seconds later she left the 'power spot'.

Like Angela, the man was curious that someone besides himself found comfort on the hill top as he did. He, too, was aware that they shared a brief and private moment seeking peace of mind. After observing the woman, it was easy to recognize the need to be respectful. He saw the woman's tears brimming in her eyes; they mirrored his own. For a few seconds, he wondered what her sorrow was about and had wanted to inquire but changed his mind. Instead, he retreated to his truck, shifted the gears from park to neutral and quietly rolled the truck down the sloping hill and disappeared.

For the first time, several years after introducing her sister Cheryl to this place of comfort and power, she wanted nothing more but to continue to introduce it to other women. So the second year after her discovery, Angela invited one of her dearest friends and college classmate from Colorado, Kathy Hayes. Kathy was visiting for the first time to attend the annual Nicodemus homecoming. That was the year the two friends made cards with Kenta cloth glued to them, as memento, for the little group of women who participated in witnessing the rising of the sun at the 'power spot'.

In 2006, six years later, after the first discovery, again the two women crafted little lapel pins to share with every woman that joined them at the power spot. The pen was symbolic of the peace she found spiritually from her mom, it was a healing that encumbered her existence! It was a delicate square piece of silk paper that was laminated and displayed two small figures holding a little flower. In the upper right corner, there was a dove to signify peace and love. The little pin was designed to represent a friendship and affirmation that the 'power spot' was a place where positive energy could be captured to comfort and mend the broken-hearted soul in search of resolution to their personal plight of grief. Eventually, they would heal and receive offerings of forgiveness from within. In turn, giving, sharing and aiding someone else in need of what they had received at the spot, by the act of being understanding and compassionate.

The pins were to be a gift Angela wanted to share with other women for several reasons. It was given as a gift of love and a reminder of the importance of loving and honoring their mothers. She had learned through her prayers that such a ritual was vital for her own heart to find peace in the relationship she would cherish forever with her mom. In spirit she wanted to let her mom know that what they shared as mother and daughter could never be replaced and would be treasured for always. It marked the first year of her foolish and misleading hindsight, if not regret, for a lack of wisdom to acknowledge her mother's strength and true love. The power of this hindsight would now be the knowledge for her to express overtly at the various power spot gatherings. This surreal and surprising discovery came from the years before her mother fell asleep in death. From this loss, she had learned to search for peace and forgiveness. It was a treasured part of her private past to share with all the women she loved, and those she had yet to know. Other women in search of relief from painful experiences in their own past.

To gain this experience of love and peace, it always would take place on a Saturday morning after the first night of the hometown celebration. This tranquil location and emotional awareness was to be shared with all the women who could attend. It seemed fitting since the morning after the late-night dancing on Friday went into the wee hours of the morning!

The time to share the favored place named the 'power spot, south of her established home in Bogue, had finally come. Little did she know that in short order the days ahead that awaited her would lead her many times to this place to fight for her battered dignity and continued love for this free land, established in 1877. Such unexpected discoveries and times would test her loyalty, honor and endurance to the ancestors that came as freed slaves to live as a free people. Secretly the 'power spot' would always be a special place she claimed as her own. Not only was there a physical connection but she found a spiritual one as well. She discovered and found a deeper desire that grew increasingly more important as time moved her forward in years. After the passing of her mother, Angela yearned for the passing days and weeks to bring her joy, to become reconciled to the essence of who she wanted to be. And that was exactly what the knowledge gained during the passage of time offered her.

The very generation in which she was a part of, all of the 4th generation descendants, had been weaved into the very fabric of history she so desperately wanted it never to be forgotten. Was that generation now standing at the crossroads of life? Once she had the time to reflect on which direction in which to go, she willingly admitted her desires had changed. Now she was inclined to live a new journey with the reality that a pure heart comes from personal honesty and truth. Going forward she wanted to capture the change and face her truth and perhaps underserved healing.

A new decade had arrived and she wanted to embrace what it would bring. Just as she was excited to embrace the last weekend of every July of each year. It represented another year to celebrate life and spiritual wisdom, also that of death and sorrow. Little did anyone know that the early morning drive to the 'power spot' of July 2010, would be different. It would be a turning point. It would be a resolution of letting go of the past to live in the present.

" GOING TO THE POWER SPOT!"

The invitation, as always, directed any able-bodied female to pow-wow at Angela's home before the light of day, to be exact, one hour before dawn. This was an absolute requirement to be up and present at her house before the sunrise. Her residence mimicked a little white cottage trimmed in sky blue from a Disney Park fantasy. It was located on the right-hand side of a dead-end street. It was easy to find. Simply make a right turn at the blinking light coming from the north, off the paved Main Street that ran straight through the small town of less than 200 residents. Bogue was the neighboring town to Nicodemus located between two state highways 24 and highway eighteen. Exactly one mile south from where the two highways connected, after crossing the Solomon River, was where the town of Bogue Kansas was located on the map.

When Angela decided to make Bogue her home, she fell in love with the little 100 year old wood frame house instantly, despite its age and that it had stood uninhabited for over ten years. Just the same, the townspeople were glad it was still stable and livable. After giving her full attention to restoring the two-bedroom one bath structure it was the most admired little house at the end of Hummingbird Lane. A dream that eventually married reality was to have a white picket fence installed. When Angela found an ad placed in the local paper regarding the sale of a used white picket fence, the transaction and exchange was pleasant. As was the owner of the fence. A tall country gentleman by the name of Steve. He was pleased that the new owner was happy that the fence would enhance her little home and offered to deliver it free of charge. Once it was painted and installed, both Angela and Steve were equally pleased with the exchange and a new found friendship. The fence was the perfect decision that complimented the manicured yard and decorative picture-perfect front porch. White oversized rocking chairs flanked either side of the bright red door with a half-moon beveled window. The house was trimmed in blue. It was small but manageable enough for her and a start to a new life. However, on this Saturday morning, all such details were unnoticed by the newcomers because of the much anticipated and early morning adventure. It was 5:00AM. Angela's little sister Priscilla, best known as PJ and her best friend, Joyce Wilson, were the first to arrive. There was no need to unlock the front door because it was a small community where everyone was trusted and watchful friends.

As PJ entered through the front door, she issued her first orders for the day. "Ladies, get up!" she demanded in an exceedingly loud voice. "Get up! Put on some clothes and shoes, and let's get this show on the road. We gotta get going to the power spot!"

Even though these instructions were given without much choice, the three sleeping figures in the house were not affected. This was indicated by several moans and groans made and heard from pillow-covered heads in the oversized bedroom.

"Get up, Girls! Moan and groan all you want. That's what you get for staying up all hours of the night!" There was no pity in her criticizing statement!

Joyce followed behind PJ into the kitchen, immediately sitting down at the antique oak table. She was still dressed in her silk pajamas and looked longingly into the bedroom, wanting nothing more than to join the other sleeping figures that captured her attention through the doorless bedroom. She knew that getting any additional sleep was a pointless topic of discussion. She redirected her attention with a smile back to PJ and continued to watch her young, lovable friend make coffee while she continued to fuss under her breath the entire time. She was annoyed because no one was following her orders and good morning instructions "To rise and shine!" which she repeated loudly several more times.

Priscilla was the youngest of seven children and was allowed to take charge of most situations for the family. This was something Joyce admired about her the most since she was the complete opposite. PJ's outspoken attitude was appreciated whenever the two women traveled places. Joyce never concerned herself about too many details; she had PJ for such things. Of course this wasn't an issue for PJ either, making the two personalities very compatible, different and completely opposite in attitudes in general. The most important complement the women owned was their mutual spirituality. This became common knowledge, after being introduced to each other at church, by Joyce's younger sister who was PJ's age, it wasn't long before they shared an endearing friendship.

Before PJ's task at hand to finish making coffee, there was a knock at the front door.

Within seconds after the rapped knock, the slightly open door popped open and there stood a newcomer.

"You made it, I don't believe it, come on in," PJ ordered in a more cheerful voice.

From the periwinkle bedroom, Angela's sleepy curiosity got the best of her. "Who is it?"

"It's Leese," Priscilla declared over her shoulder as she headed back into the kitchen.

"You guys aren't even up! My goodness. It's already starting to get light outside. I'm going back home because we're going to miss the sunrise anyway now." This declaration was made with false disappointment. I knew this should get some kind of reaction from Angela and my little cousin Teresa. I quickly gestured to PJ with a silencing finger against my smiling lips, who turned around as she was returning to the kitchen before words of dismay and protest came from her open mouth!

Joyce continued to sit in wide-eyed silence and curiosity looking from one room to the next. The coffee maker was once again back to fussing in the kitchen and wanted it to be known in mumbled expressions that it was not going to be her fault if we did not get there in time. Pointing out that she and Joyce were up before the chickens in a loud chippy voice.

That was my cue. Promptly, I made sure that the glass doorknob rattled as I opened the front door. Before I could pretend to turn and leave back out the open door, yelling and laughter, pajamas and nightgowns were flying everywhere. Dibs were given for the bathroom and I was threatened with my life if I was to leave. In short order, the coffee was forgotten and the small frame woman who had been stretched out on the sofa was told that she didn't have time to get dressed and was rushed out the front door in the oversized t-shirt used as a night shirt with everyone else. Her name was Regina. She was told to get into Angela's car. This demand was shouted into the damp morning air in the direction of the dew-covered cars.

Later, during the morning, it was explained that Regina had been invited to come for the celebrated weekend after having contacted Angela at the Historical Society in search of some unknown and additional family members. And judging from the bewildered look on her face, she knew that this was an extra special occasion that could not be missed and a one time opportunity. Before the morning adventure ended, again Regina shared that the drive from Tennessee was one she would never forget because she felt like she was "coming home!"

The other three women got into my van and wore looks of concern. It was no secret and overlooked by the local authorities most times that Angela drove from one point to the next like she was late for everything. And the best thing the locals knew to do was to keep a lookout in all directions if it was noted that her vehicle wasn't sitting in front of her house. Therefore, the girls hoped that I would have the ability to keep up with Angela, who drove her little white two-door Honda like a race car, even if she wasn't late. I had been fore-warned and was prepared to drive like I was on the freeways of Houston, Texas. Needless to say, she lived up to her reputation. Once she started the engine, we wasted not another second, headed toward Main Street and the intersection with the blinking light, turned right and headed south. As night faded away in the east, so did the paved street. In two blocks, the street turned into a chalk white sand-covered road, then it became a dusty, gravel country road that twisted and turned then curved eastward and back again until we all were heading south again, toward our destination "The power spot."

Once we arrived at the top of the highest point of a hill and out of the foggy lower landscape, the chatter that initially filled the air in both vehicles, like a group of high school girls on a scavenger hunt, subsided to a quiet hum. The quiet was as if we had all entered a local library. Deliberately departing from the two vehicles parked along the edge of the road, with cameras in tow, each car door was politely closed while we all absorbed our surroundings. Some of the looks on faces displayed odd concerns. There were voices of some sad awareness concerning the low, thick but dissipating mist as the small group of women walked to the overgrown ditch eastward, away from the parked car and my van toward the view where each could see with solemn anticipation. The concern was again on several faces. They were hopeful that there might be a chance to see the creative hand of God and a brilliant sunrise.

"This is it, girls," Angela declared, looking back and forth between the faces of the two newcomers. First from Regina's, then to my transfixed profile and back again. "You remember this place, don't you, Leese," she stated more than asked. Watching me remember tiny details from our past childhood summers. It was such a magical place of youthful enchantment!

"How could I ever forget this place?" My answer was slow and made with a pause between each word as I turned a full 360 degrees. The entire surroundings were bucolic and story-book real. My thoughts were both constant and mentally back and forth, as I experienced the memories, like a game of tug of war, from the past and back again to the present, pulled one way, then the other. For the first time I felt like I was having an out of body sensation. Floating back to face the future...when my eyes met hers...thousands of telephone conversations passed between us...once the bygone years embraced our youth and innocence. In those moments, time had no meaning; it took both of us back and forth between the decades of our childhood and now weary women of age. Past and present were mixed together to visualize fleeting images from the future. I could apprehend Angela's emotions, as she could mine from the heart. We were in silent anticipation because we both were clairvoyantly aware that the days ahead would be filled with the unknown challenges of aging a reluctant knowledge of life. Perhaps an opportunity for new beginnings before time depleted us both. For no more than brief and endearing moments in time, endless seconds in time, our eyes betrayed what we shared to be the true bond we once vowed never to forget. These vows were our promises we made as two ten-year-old little colored girls forty-two years from the past. Time might have broken our emotional feelings we shared but our promise tattered us to the future, so we couldn't forget.

"So this is the 'power spot," Regina announced, disrupting our thoughts while expressing my own feelings aloud. "This is wonderful!"

"It's more than wonderful, I just love coming here," Angela responded in a small voice.

"How did you find it?" Regina asked with curiosity.

"I first discovered it, witnessed it, felt it when I was a young teenager, when I was about fifteen. My cousin Leese and I were riding horses down that road." Angela pointed toward the abandoned buildings and overgrown roadway. In the direction toward the sloping property her deceased cousins once owned and continued to explain her story.

"It was a typical hot summer day. Skies were clear with the exception of a single bank of thunderstorm clouds building in the southwest. The sudden downpour came fast and went just as fast, quickly slowing to just a gentle sprinkle, then it quickly passed overhead to the east leaving a mist in the air and then a large rainbow appeared. Then, seconds later, a second rainbow appeared. It truly was a magnificent sight. It was my first time seeing a full rainbow as well as my first time seeing a double one at that!" Angela explained with an excited voice, looking in the direction where the event had taken place from years ago.

"I felt a surge of energy come up from the ground, and through the horse I was riding. It was as if God spoke directly to me and said, 'See my great wonders of the earth. Feel the energy of my spirit. Behold it is available to you from right here.' I remember standing tall in the saddle with my arms outstretched to the heavens, taking all the energy into my very being. I was fully charged, and something in me realized that I had a new vision, a vision that allowed me to see the world around me in a different, more vivid, energetic light!" The words rushed from Angela with excitement, as she mimicked that day with her arms stretched outward. .

"Wow!" Tereasa exclaimed, the youngest of the women and my first cousin. "I don't think I have ever heard that story before. That had to be awesome!"

Immediately, Angela replied with longing eyes, "It was and still is. Also, I know that on top of this very hill, one of the highest in the county, this is the only location where you can see five towns."

"At night you can see two more, Wakeeney and Stockton." PJ announced, and was more than eager to name the five small towns, while pointing them out the best she could across the fog filled valley.

"There is Palco, Damar, of course Nicodemus, Bogue, and Hill City, all within 360 degrees."

It was all true and fascinating because you could actually see them all from the power spot. Each little town had played a part in my life and filled my childhood journal secrets, which I was very much aware of at that moment. As the other newcomer, Regine was the most intrigued listening to each word, especially since she was hearing and being included in everything from the past for the first time. The others were watchful and quiet, preoccupied in their own thoughts. So following suit, we all became lost in our own personal feelings, secret thoughts and desires. Gazing over the horizon, the sounds of nature begin to breathe mystical sounds, like music to lift our spirits. Nature, like an orchestra of instruments, became alive as the meadowlarks sailed across the sky. A sudden cool breeze danced in and around stray wild wheat filled ditches, left behind after the harvest. The thrashing sounds of the wheat playing one against the other, provided background music to nature's natural sounds as the sun rose to kiss our faces with a bronze glow of light. We stood in single file profile waiting to receive the sun's energy, unconsciously desiring that it would give us additional hope and stronger courage. We knew that we would be forever entrusted one to the other at that very moment in time. As we stood motionless, it was easy for me to imagine the women from my living history, experiencing this same energy, now and then for the future. These were women instrumental in my past that taught me to view the future based on past experiences. After all, they were the true cornerstone women of Nicodemus. They are the wisdom from the past as memories in our present day, admiring us as we were learning to become wise women from our own plight.

Each one of us, women of age, stood quietly, almost stately. The deep rhythm from our bosoms was the only exception. The longing to see with our eyes, into the open windows of our true hearts desires was urgent. To discover and be kind to our truth...the door to our heart's freedom. For all the things hoped for and the things promised but never fulfilled. The sunrise would nurture our thoughts of the hoped for possibilites forever lost to the past, or that which could be gained once again to each of us if only in our dreams. We were strong, ready and willing to learn what the future would show us. The past of other women had taught us to fight the battles, of first being women and then especially women of every shade of color. Learning the meaning of responsibility as warriors, as protectors, as wives and mothers. Women bearing the challenge to ensure stable families during the absence of mates and companions. Naturally we made an imprint at a point in time, when we discerned that we had become the mentors from those before us to educate those we had nurtured and let go of, other women released into a world that remained shackled to a broken past.

The loss of loved ones because of the advancement of time that we couldn't control, conjured regrets and nightmares from the past and fear for the future. As mothers and teachers, we had learned there were many open windows that were never validated decisions and actions and desires were perhaps negative forces driven by history, by the past, where secrets kept in darkness, locked away in the heart of pain and sorrow. Mainly fear! And now such emotional freedom was essential...the key to release the dread from the now and future. Most importantly, this gift of awareness and light will be shared with other women like ourselves, and their future.

There we stood, weathering our own personal emotional and mental storms mature and experienced, still and silent. At my cousin's "power spot" in the middle of a white chalked country road on a hilltop south of a small town called Bogue in Northwestern Kansas. This "power spot" was a place where a soul could be fed spiritual consciousness, a place to strengthen the mind and a place to heal broken hearts! This was a place that could be shared and given to others held dear and close to the heart, women in need of understanding and loving guidance. This was just one of the discernments over the years, Angela was learning to accept in her own life, realizing also other women continuiously lived in hiding and fraught with their personal flights and struggles, which were so similar to her own. It could be compared to peering into a mirror most times and seeing the need to be empowered women and offer that same gift to others no different than ourselves. The aftermath of this experience stemmed more from the promotion of unguarding the heart, and was the conduit that eased the open confidentiality of hidden secrets!

Later, in the days ahead, after we left the spot that day, it became clear with acute understanding why this location to Angela had become such a necessary place to visit on countless occasions throughout the year. She found her mother's love there, appreciating the life she lived with understanding, accepting and learned the value of even forgiving herself, to treasure what was most valuable, the love her mother had for her. This newfound awareness provided the peace she found in a spiritual sense as well, to love herself. It was necessary and tied to her survival to live on the high plains near her beloved hometown of Nicodemus.

As it has done for egons, the morning ebbed it's way into a new day and we remained quietly motionless and watched the sun flood the sky with its brilliant light. In no order of age or stature we stood, in a zigzagged formation facing each of our own anticipations with a willingness to share our secrets and surrender our hearts and speak openly to the sunrise. It's prominant markings of orange, yellow and crimson sphere rising above the fog-induced landscape announced that morning was ascending, beginning to crest the horizon and expose a new day, a new beginning. This was our collective and unspoken hope, was a "new beginning."

In the now silent morning, a voice informed the distant landscape, "I don't remember ever seeing fog like this in the past?"

Another voice, "I don't either."

Then the first voice again, "At least not for the past ten or twelve years, not since we first came here." Even though Angela's voice came first, followed by Teresa's, clearly they were not speaking to one another. A new voice almost whispered the next question.

"I wonder what it means?" I did not recognize the sound that seemed to escape from my mouth in search of clarity. There was no response. Clearly, the tune of the question gave way to silence, in the form of private meditation, to silence and the sounds of nature. The question, like that moment in time, hung in the air as did the milky mysterious fog in the valley beneath the brilliance of the rising sun.

Superstitions had long left my beliefs of daily existence. Once knowledge of true spiritual guidance empowers your mind and reasoning ability, things that happen much of the time are usually based on behavior and desires. People's questionable decisions are sometimes guided or even miss-guided by uncertainty. Or simply being aware of fear and the unknown, can also be culprits. But just once, from a child's wish, I wanted to believe that the "fog" was there because of my dad. I wanted the fog to be his farewell message just for me. It was a glance at my first private and fleeting thoughts as the sun peeked into my soul and glowed upon my weary body. My true meditations were captured by the reality of all the other invitations I had ignored or missed, to be here and face the wonder and insufficient existence of who we are on the face of this earth. And yet, how fortunate we all must be to be here, thankful to our creator for the chance to view his majesty in the sunrise of life.

The beauty of our circular surroundings kept my heart from becoming heavy at that precise moment. I wanted this moment in time, just a few moments longer, to be about me and not my father. I remember feeling selfish and child-like at that instant. Perhaps I was more exhausted from my sorrow than I wanted to admit. It seemed odd that the previous week, on a Saturday, long after the sun announced itself and hung low in the afternoon sky, I said my final goodbye to my daddy in the rearview mirror as I drove from the cemetery. The dust from the cars that followed through the wooden gates swallowed the steel gray box that held my daddy from my view. Similar to the fog that lay above the trees, on the sloping hillside where I now stood alone. I didn't want to share my father's passing with anyone, at that moment. So I forged a peaceful heart and refused to cry and continued to marvel at the endless horizon and wished for my childhood one more time in my life.

I knew it was a special moment as I stood and reminisced about my selfishness, watching the sun slowly draft above the fog, slightly higher above the landscape. There were seven of us who shared those brief moments locked in a circle with our hands to express our promises. I did not know that it was part of the ritual of coming to the power spot. So I listened carefully, searching the faces of each person, watching their eyes fill with pain and relief as their voices drifted away into the morning air. I remember Johnine, my first cousin who had arrived later, declaring she was sure 'seven' had something to do with the bible and completeness.

"Precisely, spiritually speaking, it does," I stated. Then we each shared our promise once a talking stick with the silver butterfly was passed one to the next. Mine were last but simple. I wanted my promises to be thought provoking, to have meaning, to stimulate thinking ability, so the words of wisdom could be deposited in the heart for the days ahead. "Don't ignore your intuition, it is an invitation that could change your whole life. Be kind to your truth. It can be your freedom from the fears of the past." Then we bowed our heads in personal private prayers.

In those unspoken minutes, where we stood together and alone that day, we captured the secrets of our hearts in the brilliance of the sun's rays. After the sun dawned in the sky and floated just above the horizon, we became animated once again. Alive and giddy, like schoolgirls on their continued adventure. We all wanted to possess the disposition of how we had been on our way to the "power spot." Full of anticipation and excitement to pledge ourselves to make the future a new beginning. Even though our discovery was solemn at first, because the light of the suns' illumination was camouflaged by the fog. What we needed to see but weren't able to, or simply were not able to discern was in fact in plain sight. That this very day that we stood in would mark the embodiment of our individual plights. Securing our past, our history with hope and lessons learned to stabilize our future without regrets…that would become our history lesson.

In that instant, there was a peculiar draw for me to separate from the others. I wanted to capture photos and frame them so they wouldn't fade from my aging memory. With quick steps, I walked along the disappearing roadway to get a better view of the deteriorating buildings where I once visited as a young girl, to ride horses and hike into the surrounding valleys. At every opportunity, we were in search of the rock tables, where natural spring water flowed clean and fresh. To set and drink the gift from the earth at this now unforgettable abandoned homestead!

Like most places in the area, time drained the life from these family settlements one of two ways, economically or by death! I quickly suppressed the once happy images of long ago. I felt it necessary to save them for another time, another visit to this place with a more joyful and carefree heart. My need this morning was to capture the now and here on film for my heart and in my adult mind. The remaining structures in the distance appeared like shadows and silhouettes on a movie set consumed by time and foliage beyond the narrowing overgrown driveway. The remains of the boarded-up house and a couple of sheds were dwarfed by the barn that provided endless Huck Finn and Tom Sawyer summer fun! My longing for the past was painful, bittersweet as the expression goes;, unexpectedly, tears filled my eyes.

Side by side, my little cousin Teresa and I, who had followed after me, walked back to where the others stood, occupied in conversation. At that moment, we all moved towards the ditch to let an approaching SUV pass. Instead it pulled over. Johnine, the late comer, climbed out of the vehicle with her usual grim on her face. She always smiled. It just was one of her natural delightful qualities. This time it was playful for being late to the party!

The first words out of her mouth were directed towards me. "I just knew you would make it this time" she said in a little tearful voice as we hugged each other as if we were long lost friends.

After a playful squeeze to her face my comment was informative. "When I drove by the bed and breakfast, I thought about stopping, but I didn't see your car, so instantly I thought you were already at Angela's. So I kept going."

"No. The girls and I are staying at Thomas's house instead of his B&B, along with Sharon and her daughter."

As for listeners, Angela was the only one that joined in the conversation. "Where is Sharon Wellington, thought she was coming with you, she told me she wanted to come out here."

"She told me to go ahead and that she would have to make it another time because she didn't want to make me late even though I was already late anyway." Then Johnine turned to capture the last of the rising sun. Then she looked back again over her shoulder at the rest of us; her curious eyes settled on mine again with a solemn look and shared her thoughts, "It feels different." She rubbed the invisible shivers from her exposed arms. Johnine continued to express her thoughts aloud with questions to anyone that wanted to reply.

"Where did all the fog come from? Did anyone notice that there are seven of us here? I wonder what the number seven really means. Doesn't it have spiritual meaning?"

"Precisely," I stated. There wasn't a verbal response from the others. We all knew it meant something and this place had changed our lives forever. I found the number of women interesting as well, sure that the number carried some kind of meaning to the seven of us. But for now, it didn't have to mean anything in particular. Of the seven, two were sisters, three were first cousins, and these five were all relatives. The sixth guest was the youngest sister's friend, and the last woman was there in search of a family connection. The roots and history of her life had directed her here to our "little all black town." The two visitors, as it were, also bore the burden of losing loved ones and were in need of healing. They also felt the blanket of love and witnessed the power of kinship that could have been lost if not for the research and determination of one woman.

The present, this moment, this experience that placed the seven of us here together will never be forgotten. The words spoken and shared will mold and keep our actions focused on living in the future, with wisdom and acute appreciation. Of course, our intellectual awareness was alerted to the fact that however empowering rituals such as this one, they didn't offer "do overs." We had to move forward with wisdom and trust in our discoveries of honesty, humility and prayerful guidance into the future.

"Before we go, we have always let God know what we feel in our hearts or anything else that we have to let him know so he can help us achieve our hearts desires.." After Angela announced this statement, she held out a round smooth piece of drift wood attached to a silver decorative bangle butterfly bracelet to Regina on her right. Then we all naturally shared our words from the heart as it was passed to each of us.

Each of our thoughts were similar but different and attached to becoming determined with renewed faith and burden-free from the past as mature women. Once again, we stood quietly in a circle with receptive hearts to listen and capture the expressions of truth offered openly to our heavenly Father. Our words were terms of endearment and entitled sunrises that would bond our union, one to the other. We were all in total agreement to preserve this moment, this special day within our written declarations. The suggestion came from Angela after we had finished with our brief speeches. We would each write down what we had just experienced.

Johnine then pointed to me and said, "Glue it all together in a story, Leese baby." (Yet another nick-name from our Uncle Harold, one of my dad's younger brothers.) I, in turn, remained silent and felt such a great privilege that she felt I should pen this experience. I was shy to admit that I hadn't written anything in years. Each of us wrote our personal thoughts and desires. Appropriately, the beginning belonged to Angela's sunrise, so I felt in my heart, because it was what all of our sunrises were based upon, it should be called "An Awakening!"

Angela's Sunrise

"The Awakening"

When I thought about it, at first I thought it was like the sun coming up on the eastern horizon. Like the sun, making its daily grand entrance to light up the magnificent worldly landscape on which God has created his wonders. Like the light gray clouds hiding the sun's rays or rays reflecting just a bit of light through the canopy of thick summer fog lacing the prairie weeds, bushes, and trees in the valley. I thought it was like the first bright rays streaking across the vast open sky announcing yet another day. About how six other women were seeing this natural daily wonder, high on a lonely hill in the middle of a dusty dirt road six miles from the nearest town. About how I had done this so many times before, all by myself, on this same little spot. A power spot to me, and that's what I call it. How the first time I brought another woman with me, my sister Cheryl, and then officially the first gathering of women a year later with my friend Kathy and a few others. I thought about it, then couldn't remember how long it had actually been, but I think it was 1998 when we first met the morning sun on my favorite spot on earth. "Mine," now our power spot.

Yes, this is what I first thought when I thought about writing about "sunrise." Then…

I stopped thinking about it. And a few days ago Johnine called and asked what we were supposed to write about. This got me thinking again, but this time "sunrise" didn't make me think of those same things that day of the gathering. This time I was bombarded with the real sunrise that is happening at this time in my life. These are the words and concepts that kept popping up as I think about "sunrise" now.

Awaking…..that's what it is – it's my awakening from the last six years of constant grief. Awaking from a dense fog, like the first time of oppressive grief. Functioning. I was but grief stricken even more profoundly from the death of my mother five years before. I was awaking to a world where I had obviously been asleep. As I have been waking up to the world, I had neglected from my thoughts the reality of the world around me. I could see that I had been asleep. When I first opened my eyes, as I was waking, I could see things had changed. I could see it in the wrinkles of the familiar faces around me. When did they get "that" old-looking? The answer was clear, when I was asleep. Where were those that seem so familiar to me and a "take it for granted" they'll always be here. Some had passed, and I couldn't remember when. I couldn't remember because I was asleep. How did those nieces and nephews, cousins and friends get so big, so grown? When I was asleep. Where had some gone – moved on, moved away, or simply just left the area. When I was asleep. When did Barrie lose his teeth and start wearing dentures? Dad slept too many hours in his chair, TJ start working in Quinter, Reggie leave Nicodemus for Cincinnati, they find oil on my land, Floppy (a dog that showed up on my front door stoop one day, out of nowhere) get gray hair and half blind, when going to Hays only happens once every two or three weeks? When did my hair get so thin, my fat start hanging, half of my teeth fall out, asthma get so bad, eat more than I've ever eaten, miss having a man around? When did all this happen, I kept thinking. When I was asleep?

When I opened my eyes to the morning of my new life, I began to realize that I had been asleep. Now that I am awake and the dream has finally revealed itself as my sleep walking, or I might even say sleep living, I don't want to forget that I was sleeping and now I am awake. Wide-eyed but awake! I don't have to continue to sleepwalk in grief. I can visit the good times gone by with those I have lost, and all I have to do is remember them. I can greet each sunrise with the knowledge that I am wide awake and no longer have to sleepwalk in grief. I can breathe the morning fresh air and know that I am awake and alive, no longer sleeping in grief.

I'm awake and can witness the morning sun rising above the eastern horizon and share that moment with kindred sisters. I am awake and want to live this day, and each day that the sun rises, I am blessed to see it. I am awake, alive, no longer asleep. I'm still here to live the rest of my life, each day at a time. I'm awake to witness the sunrise once again. Awake, wide awake! And so I see the sunrise with joy and peace and with the knowledge that I am awake to see it in all its glory.

Angela Bates, 8/2010

Johnine's Sunrise

"ANTICIPATION"

Sunrise 2010 had to get there, even if I was late. I have teased Angela that we didn't need to be there at the spot until 6:15 at least. So I wouldn't have to get up so early. Knowing when my day began, I would be busy the entire day until after the fashion show without a break. I felt bad. I didn't wake Sharon up early enough to go to the power spot. I could be late or go on by myself. She told me to go ahead. Took off in the suv, trying to remember which turn in the road to take. I looked down the street toward Angie's house, but they were already gone, so I headed south, passed the cemetery, and passed the first left road and decided it didn't curve to the left as I remembered so I kept going, trying to get there before the sun came up. Took the second left and then took the first right to go south up and down over the hills, and couldn't see anyone or anything. The fog was terrible. Kept going, had to get there. What did I miss? (It was explained that the fog looked like floating clouds, symbolic, leaving as the sun tried to break through for a new day.)

Got there, drove up, all stopped, looked around, and moved to the side of the road, but I pulled up and stopped. They saw who it was and said yes, she got here. Who is present is the core of this history to move it forward, from this present point in time, to our future? We would take our family to the future. The excitement of getting to the power spot to get re-energized for another year would be a blessing. After homecoming 2009, we lost our main family root, Grandma Ora, and this year, her oldest child, my Uncle Boo (Freddie)! I felt the void this year. I felt so detached as I participated in the various activities from homecoming. Still going through the motions of loss. As they say, the show has to keep going, even if it's altered from the players in actions, it goes on. Before a year is up, our oldest uncle Freddie died two weeks before homecoming, before he got recognized for being a great baseball player. Veryl (his youngest brother) is not the only famous athlete in the family. Uncle Boo hit a baseball off of Satchel Paige. Every baseball player can say that.

The circle of prayer formed with us present with us being hands length around the circle to begin our sharing of prayers, words of encouragement, comments, and feelings. I commented after we had all shared our thoughts that unconsciously how our circle had closed to a smaller one. We as family and friends made a tighter circle as we grew closer together as a natural movement to get close to each other through this power bond; we have shared our feelings and even over the years since 1998. I haven't made all the sunrises, but I have made several of them. My feelings are that I was always afraid I would oversleep and miss it.

(What has been my contribution?) I know Beans and Jeans was my vision three years ago to start off HC with a meet and greet for those who came early to kick off HC. Every year we try to come up with something new and to add to it. Beans, corn bread, meat, cookies, beer, lemonade, Fritos, who knows where our menu will end in 2011. New people, family friends, guests, big suggestions, homecoming is taking on a new look; we will have to embrace it, or we will be left behind. It will not only look different but feel different. The Williams, Wellington and Switzer family have seen a year different than any before. We or I can't close our eyes to change. We or I have to get with the changes that are happening before our and my eyes. Not saying I like it, but the choice is limited, so embrace it and be a part of it (my head was full of ghosts and images, past and present).

The sun broke through as a new day began, one that wasn't ever promised to any of us. We received a gift of "a new day, a new homecoming," in 2010.

Imagine if you will, the first weekend in July 1877. The conversation going on in the township of Nicodemus, just what kind of celebrating would there be doing? Being surrounded with special food, friends, family, and fellowship. Who was driving over from closer townships to let the good times roll? Was there dancing, jitterbugging, auctions off of women and baskets of food to have a special or private picnic? Did they have cake walks? Dessert walks? Is there a record of what the first homecoming was composed of?

Was special fabric ordered from the mercantile? For a new dress, watermelon seed spitting contest. Bake off contest. The annual talent shows? What did they do on their first homecoming? (I must know the beginning of it all.)

I learned during HC 8-2010——-Williams, Wellington, Switzer women are strong, smart, independent women. Marriage, yes, we believe in the bond of marriage. Any brother coming to pursue a woman from our family, they need to bring a well dressed table. In other words, don't come half steppin. The women in our family are well-educated and have skills to run homes and companies (And fry the bacon all at the same time). So if you dare come with some "booty" as in the back-country. Bring it to the table with all the trimmings (or don't come at all!). We play hard and love gentle to the fullest. We take care of business and family and have very strong spiritual beliefs. So why do we end in divorce? For various reasons, the men chose to leave or do stupid things that remove themselves personally, or they choose not to pay the rent or mortgages. When the men fail to do what the heads of families are expected to do, then they have to GO! Till death do we part, yes, but if the men fail at leadership, they go; they have met with their own defect. Sometimes a woman is the woman to do what needs to be done. We know how to be submissive to our husbands and mates, but we won't put up with stupidity! Education is a good thing to have. We will use it when necessary to achieve our goals and to reach expectations to succeed in life. To be ready for every sunrise!

Johnine Powell, August 2010

Teresa's Sunrise

"Solitude"

As we all gathered at our "special" place, and again we were able to see the sunrise one more time, I always went back to being a child, lying in the bed upstairs in the east room. There I would listen to the chickens clucking and the rooster crowing, the birds singing, and Grandma downstairs getting breakfast ready for the "boys." A cool breeze would sometimes come in the morning, wafting over me as I listened to the deep voices downstairs talk about going out in the fields, how the crops are doing, or when will we get rain. The grease sizzled as Grandma fried up the ham and bacon or any other meat that she might happen to have had. Percolating coffee aroma would snake up the stairs, making me hungry for the taste, though years later when I actually had coffee, I was amazed to find how bitter it tasted! I leaped out of bed to go downstairs so I could spend some time with my dad, uncles, and Grandpa. I enjoyed listening to them, especially in the morning; they laughed and joked, passing the biscuits and sand plum jelly, eating at a fast pace, getting ready to meet the day head on. Every once in a while, you could hear the deep throat chuckle of either Grandma or Grandpa in response to what Dad or his brothers, Freddie T., Lee, and occasionally Harold would say. They would actually complement each other; Grandpa's deep rough chuckle always showed the inner boy in him and Grandma's smooth deep contralto that showed an inner girl that made you wonder what she was like when she was young. It was the best part of them, which made me want to make them laugh more often, just so I could get that glimpse. Then they were done, the men ready to go start their day with lunch pails and jugs in hand. Grandpa usually trailed, with one or more dogs tagging behind, stepping in that old green Ford truck with visors looking like Grandpa's eyebrows. Inside Grandma was getting ready for the next crew: the women and the children. That time was special to be alone with Grandma and just being quiet. We shared many quiet moments together over the years, sharing conversations, taking naps together, or just talking. Now there is only

Dad and Harold left from those early morning breakfasts and a public pancake feed that is part of the celebration. The last two years have seen the loss of the anchors of our small community, however, when I come to see the sunrise, I am instantly placed back into a time where I hear Grandpa chuckling with his dogs by his side, Prince Albert in the front pocket of his overalls. I see once again Uncle "Boo" and Uncle Lee bantering back and forth at the kitchen table, laughing at how I ate the variety of meats like a "true country girl." Grandma worked in a small kitchen like it was a commercial kitchen in a restaurant. As well as Mom and Aunt 'Nita talking with Aunt Lorene and Aunt Avalon while Grandma looks on to see that her table, her family, her life had been infinitely blessed.

Teresa Switzer, August 2010

Priscilla's Sunsire
"I Grieve"

July 31st, 2010 5:36 A.M.

I Grieve

I grieve as I look at the rolling hills that tumble to Nicodemus.

Many ancestors have come and gone, leaving their imprints upon the land but importantly leaving us our wonderful rich history of the past and of the things to come.

Yes, I grieve as I am standing here on the power spot looking at God's precious beauty of the land before my eyes. Energy flowing through and out my body, enveloping me to cry out for the unknown but the peace that be stills my heart. I look to the heavens, giving thanks to God who has made it possible for the things that have come in and out of my life as tears of joy, tears of sadness, and tears of pain emerge from deep within my soul.

Gazing to the east as the sun begins to rise across the horizon, brilliant, huge of iridescent color, so bright that it brings tears to the eyes when looking directly from a far. It continues to rise as every living creature God has created comes to life.

The eagle soars from the west; the birds chirp as they fly pass, the bugs awake, and the cows moo as this glorious moment of sunrise begins.

God and his angels simply tune the universe, no matter how far across the sea, for when the sun rises, the sun will set and the Father spreads his loving arms, welcoming all his children home, especially his setting sun.

Priscilla (PJ) Bates, 8/2010

Joyce's Sunrise
"Thankful"

It still rings in my ears, "Let's commit to finishing one thing before we move to the next project." It was a statement made by Johnine. I had to and wanted to agree with her. Being with these women, I really didn't know but one well but felt connected to them somehow, making me aware of my family. How important that each member within that structure should be in my life. The ones that have fallen asleep in death will never know in this lifetime the value they hold in my heart. I miss them, and at the same time I want to tell the ones that are alive and will while I can the depth of my love! I believe that all of us are connected because of the spirit of God and the spirit of our loved ones he holds in his blossom.

As I stood with my other sisters on the mesa overlooking Nicodemus, taking in the sight of God's majesty, it dawned on me how much we humans take for granted that he is worthy to be praised. Every element that our finite minds and eyes could take in still did not reveal God's total glory.

I stood thanking him for the new family that had been formed the weekend before. The marriage of my great nephew Cameron and his bride Desiree for the new family God had created. How much more we all longed for loved ones now gone to have been there. Missing was his grandmother, Donna. How much more grateful we would have been to praise God, if our sister Shirley and his great-grandmother Queen Esther and our mother. Her sister Audrey, and of course, great-great-aunts Bernice, Effie, and Uncle Theodore were physically present. Somehow we knew their spirits were with us on that day, as they are here with me now.

Being grafted into Nicodemus, via the Bates family, I also felt that these people that came to settle this Kansas land were also my true ancestors. I felt the struggles that they had to endure and their triumphs over adversity. Everything that has breathed praises the Lord.

2 Corinthians 4:7-10 sums it all up for the seven women that stood on that hill.

> *"We who have this spiritual treasure are like common clay pots, to show that the supreme power belongs to God, not to us. 8.We are often troubled, but not crushed; sometimes in doubt, but never in despair; 9. there are many enemies, but we are never without a friend; and though badly hurt at times, we are not destroyed. 10. At all times we carry in our mortal body the death of Jesus, so that his life also may be seen in our bodies."*

So to myself and my six sisters that stood there with me, we can say, as a people, still we raise.

Joyce Wilson, 8/2010

Regina's Sunrise
"The Fantasy"

Nicodemus was just a fantasy in my mind before I actually experienced it. I told my cousin Angela that I was going to come to the next "homecoming" five years ago when I met her over the internet and discovered we were related. Our relationship has grown immensely over the years, as she would come to Nashville to speak or be close enough for me to meet her in Kentucky. But the reality of going didn't seem that feasible each year when it was time to attend "homecoming." I, however, always looked forward to her coming this way. We could always find conversations and interests in common; we have come to realize that we are more like blood sisters.

But this year, when she extended the invitation, I jumped at it. I don't know if it was because I was just making excuses before or if I just didn't think it would be something that I would truly enjoy. Nonetheless, I was going this time. I had heard about the good times and about all of the people who attend each year, families connecting and friends who just want to be a part of the celebration. The history that I was so much a part of was lying out in a part of Kansas that made it almost impossible to think how my ancestors braved the unknown to finally call this place called Nicodemus home.

So I took off to a territory unknown to me and much to my surprise, the five-hour drive from the Kansas City airport was enjoyable, and I began to feel the excitement grow as I traveled Interstate-70, experiencing the beautiful Flint Hills and countryside…and to all the folks who reminded me before I left that Kansas was boring and flat. I began to wonder, what road did they travel? The green rolling hills and wide-open land made me feel like this ride was going to be alright as I turned my stereo up and danced all the way to WaKeeney, Kansas. LOL… forty minutes past my turn off. Oh well, that just gave me a reason to see a road I might not have traveled. I got a thrill when I finally pulled up to this beautiful blue cottage at the end of Hummingbird Lane where I was getting ready to see my cousin Angela! What a quaint place with the charm of someone who knows how to make her house feel like HOME...it was time to celebrate, and so we talked, ate, and giggled until the wee hours in the morning.

The visit to the only visible "dug-out" was humbling and overwhelming all at the same time. Emotions filled in my veins as I realized and confirmed that our ancestors actually lived in the side of hills! I took pictures but didn't have the nerve to want to get closer. It humbled me to see this in real time. Tears fell as I imagined how it might have been during that first brutal Kansas winter.

Now to fast forward to the actual "Emancipation celebration." I was beside myself when I finally arrived in Nicodemus! As the crowds grew each day, I reminded myself that though my folks from the Thomas and Smith clan had made this their final destination some 132 years ago from Kentucky, that their seeds were still planted here. Any and everybody I saw reminded me of someone in my own family, and I began to feel the closeness...and oh, what about those BUFFALO SOLDIERS?

The surprising and all too emotional treat that I had on this journey was finding the gravesite of my great-great grandmother, Minerva Bradford Smith. Thanks to the internet, I was able to search and discern that she and my grandfather, Granville (aka Grandison), were possibly some of the first settlers here in Nicodemus who were located on an 1880 census.

As I searched through records at the Hill City Historical society, the very helpful clerk helped me to find her name, as well as her burial plot in the Hill City Cemetery – Block 11, Lot 15, and Space 7. Wow, I am getting ready to confirm what would have seemed only a dream yesterday is actually getting ready to become a reality. When I received directions, I hurried to get there to finally meet her. Now with less than two miles outside Hill City, I arrived and went almost directly to the spot that she would lay. Chills and emotions rushed through me as if I was really going to see her! I counted off the spaces and confirmed it by the map; I have finally found her. If I could only see her face or an inkling of how she might have behaved. Could I possibly look like her or have ways like her? The rush was too much, so I gently laid my hand upon her head where a stone should be and we talked, and I promised her that I would look for her in heaven! There's no marker here, so I made a mental note to make sure that the resting place would not remain unmarked. This venture made it all worth this trip, what a satisfying accomplishment. I felt cleansed.

Seeing the "vintage" baseball game finally become one of Angela's dreams come true, made it even more exciting. You could see the exhilaration all over her face that day. She worked so tirelessly, and it surely paid off. The spectators had a fabulous time, and the game was loads of fun. Isn't it great to fulfill a dream?

The pinnacle of my stay was that Saturday morning "sunrise" experience. Angela had told me about it many times before, and I was so eager to experience it. I can't say that I am an early morning person by any stretch of the imagination, but I went to bed late that night in hopes that we wouldn't miss this event.

Sure enough my "sisters" came rapping at the door at 5:00 A.M. all excited! The task of getting ready didn't seem to be as daunting this particular morning as most mornings. I was going to join the sisterhood on sunrise hill!

As we began our trek a few miles up a dusty road in our pajamas (that was cool!), I saw to my right two white-tailed deer jumping into the wilderness. Wow, how incredible is nature? We quickly arrived at our destination, which probably took no more than ten minutes, and then a magic came over me that I began to get goose bumps on my goose bumps! The quiet, peaceful, landscape was almost too stunning to take in all at once! The fog set upon the slopes like a milky waterway as the sun peeked its head above the horizon, the birds began to sing and dance as if to say, "IT'S A NEW DAY, GET UP AND LET'S CELEBRATE!" The cows in a distance started to moo a song that sounded like they were joining the birds in this morning dance...and then as the sun rushed it's bright head above the far-off sky, I at once felt its warmth and splendor upon my body, I felt the closeness of God and all His majesty! My sisters were feeling it, too... and we marveled at this occurrence that we all shared together...and it was good!

That morning on "power hill," I felt honored to have shared this moment and precious time with six of my "new sisters," and as we prayed, I felt the sense of a renewed spirit and an affirmation in my heart that all that mattered was that I was here, with my family...and it was then that I had this feeling of being baptized all over again....

Regina Thomas, 8/2010

Earlice's Sunrise
"The Invitation"

The first thought that came to mind was that I was thankful for accepting the invitation to come to this place after missing all the other times. The experience of seeing the mystic sunrise overlaid with the fog possessed many meanings for me. The first thing to always remember and practice was to never become bitter or revengeful at heart. For good reason, I had learned that out of the heart comes the sources of a person's life. The second was to live life as an honest-hearted person when dealing with other individuals. It was what I wanted each woman to take with them by verbally depositing my expressions of hopes into their hearts. They were words learned and taught to me by other women of Nicodemus, words of experience and wisdom. "Don't ignore your God-given sense of intuition; it's wisdom that could change your whole life. Be kind to your truth. It can be your freedom from the fears of the past." They weren't my mother's exact words, but I took them to heart and wanted to share them. I was the last to share my thoughts after the sunrise out of the seven women then we bowed our heads in private personal prayer. It was in that instant of bowing my head that I found myself in Wichita Kansas, standing on an empty street at one-thirty in the early morning hours praying to Jehovah God and being thankful for his guidance and peace of mind.

I remembered so clearly leaving the hotel, across the street from the hospital, that served as housing for those visiting family members no different than myself. I hurried across the middle of the street to the hospital where my dad had been life-flighted, almost two and half years before his death. Visiting hours were just about over and our mom wanted to stay for as long as she could with the 'Old Man'(something I fondly called him) until visiting hours were over. Between the two of us girls, my sister Norma and myself we managed to hide the fact that Norma was sick with a high fever and I had forged the assumption that she would entertain all of the waiting room guests, until they all had left, staying clear of the ICU area. Once everyone had left to go home or to their hotel rooms, we quickly made our way to the hotel to get her medicated and into bed. My concern was that she had a fever of 102. I felt bad having to leave her; I had no other choice. I had to hurry back to the hospital to check on our dad's prognosis from the night nurse and retrieve our weary mother. Once I received the update on his condition, I was reminded that he was not out of the woods by any means. We left his room and went straight to the ER. The ICU Nurse on duty had voiced her concerns about my mom's irregular heartbeat and suggested that I get her checked-out downstairs in the ememergy room. After getting her checked-in and paperwork completed, I could see the fatigue in her eyes and that she was exhausted with worry. When the ER attendant came to retrieve her for an additional test, we both made it a point of reassuring each other vocally, also with hugs and a kiss. I was told to relax because it would take about 45 minutes for a complete examination. As soon as the wheelchair disappeared behind the oversized doors, I left the hospital and hurried back to the hotel. Once there, I found Norma shivering with a higher fever of 103. I had hoped that the fever would have gone down to at least 100 degrees. When I asked how she felt the response was a mumble...that she would be fine. I repeated all of the treatments from when I first put her into bed, covered her with all the blankets I could find, and forced her to drink extra water and to take an extra fever reducing pill. As soon as I had entered the room, when I first arrived, I cranked up the heat and now it was unbearably hot, but this helped her stop shivering. Her breathing was slow and steady and the forehead test proved that there was a slight drop in her temperature. I was so very thankful because I only had a few minutes before I needed to return to the ER to check on 'BeBe', our mother (yet another nickname given to her by me when I was twelve).

Once I was sure I had the room key in hand, I left the room and hurried back to the hospital. My heart began to beat rapidly as I thought of both my parents being sick and the possibility of losing either one of them. I hurried out of the hotel and began to cry. As I was crossing the street in the quiet of the night, I suddenly just stopped in the middle of it. The ER light was no longer on above the glass doors. It paralized me in my tracks. All I could do was stand still and beg God for help.

Then like out of a movie, large snowflakes started to fall from the black sky. I was almost covered instantly as I brushed them from my face. The falling snowflakes were beautiful and peaceful as was my pounding heart. Then a horn blared and jilted me back to awareness and the reality that I was standing in the middle of the street at 1:00 in the morning. I fostered forgiveness with a single wave of my hand and continued across the street into the glass doors to find my mom coming out of the examination room fully dressed with paperwork in hand. Our eyes shared a moment of love and relief.

As we left the hospital ER arm-in-arm she asked one simple question. "How is your sister, is she better?" In response, all I could do was take her hand into mine while shaking my head yes. She's a mom, our mom. Of course she was aware of our little secret. One more time I was thankful and when I raised my head from my prayer, I viewed the rising sun one more time.

Simutantiously, all seven of us ended our private prayers with hugs for each other and the wonderful journey of awareness and peace we found from sharing the experience together while watching a Kansas sunrise.

Several days later, I could not get the moment spent with six other women out of my thoughts. Nor could I shake that my intuition was forcing me to seek solace in the confines of my house. Little did I realize just how much my life had changed and little did I comprehend that my dad's passing, the darkest moment for me, would ironically be a light that brought me straight out of a state of mindless existence. I spent fifteen hours, after leaving my hometown, on the open highway thinking that I was being pulled by a black asphalt road to safety. It was a lifeline pulling me further away from my anxiousness and toward the overwhelming and growing need to hide inside my house. I had a one-track mind. Once I got home everything would be okay, my desires were wishful thinking. I hoped everything would be alright. I was running away from what I had just experienced. Death! I did not know that the reality of it would leave me paralyzed. I had been living on autopilot, going through the necessary motions to survive my own personal fears of failure. I had wrapped myself in a winter blanket for all the seasons of the year and pretended that I was alright. I pretended that my M.O.

was normal, that I was not cold when I felt the frost of life or that I wasn't exhausted from the heat of anger and fear. But it was all tied to my grief!

Once inside my dimly lit and empty house, void of any other soul, the silence gripped my senses like the most dangerous forces of nature. The one sure protector in my life had fallen asleep in death and I was brokenhearted. The one saving factor I was sure of in my weary anticipated days ahead was my mom. She was always a safe place of comfort, trustworthy, and a protector for the broken-hearted. She was beyond reliable and possessed a profound steadfast love. But for now, as I had prayed, my safe haven was not within the confines of a structure made of wood and stone, behind the walls where I lived for so many years, as apart of a family unit. "Home" and the security that I was desperate to run to was not in my house. It was the serenity of my mind, heart, and soul. It was to simply live in the present, the right now and fight my nightmares with spiritual guidance and help. I was my safe place; I was my home! Finally I was waking up to my sunrise. I could be selfish in my nudity, a rebirth as it were. It was just me, and me alone for the first time in my life. There was no spouse to welcome home and no child to coddle. For an hour, I sat perfectly still on the floor against my fireplace, holding a single key to my house and watched without sight the realities of a forgone life with a clear mindset, of a new beginning and the blessings of a Kansas sunrise.

> "I sat with my anger long enough until she told me her real name was Grief." *C.S.Lewis*
>
> Earlice "Leesa" Switzer-Rupp, August 2010.

"THE SUNSET"

I have always enjoyed how the sunset beckons the iridescent colors of night fall with its shadows and outlines that gradually fade under a blanket of a black starry sky. It is truly mesmerizing how such a great and powerful luminary as the sun can disappear into darkness. And with all it's glory brings us into a new brilliant sun-filled day. It is an **awakening** to yet another day with a different viewpoint on life. With hopes to heal from the warmth when the beaming rays of morning offer a "do over." Yet, there is only one day that we can live and that is the one in which we dwell, where choices are made that become our past after the sunset. So with each choice that we attach our ***anticipation*** upon, in our life choices, the opportunity could slip away if we do not stay prepared and sanction those precious moments. Moments perhaps, that can draw us from an existence of ***solitude*** and assuming there is no one that can utterly understand the nucleus of our hearts, the joy we may experience, and especially the ***grief*** that can damage our faith. Therefore, we anxiously hope for our desires and dreams to bring a different kind of day. So before the day ahead of us begins, we are ***thankful*** and find that most endearing sense of love through the friendships we find in each other nevertheless each day we live and envision the future. And yes, it is okay to want the next day to bring us peace, the same peace that we request to be given us in our desires and prayers! This is how we know the life we have been given, each of us, is not a ***fantasy:*** anyone of us may discover throughout a day, as we stand and give glory to the heavens in our darkest moments in time, an open door to live life with appreciation and a positive attitude yet again. So, before the days slip away and the present marries the future, that which will produce our past, look for the ***invitation*** to live, love, and explore the joy of life before the sunset.

After sharing that day on a country hilltop road watching the rising sun, for over a decade that moment was treasured and tucked away like a beloved keepsake, saved and seldom mentioned again by the seven women collectively. It wasn't a forbidden memory. It just seemed appropriate and private for the time being. Those cherished minutes would be sustaining for the days ahead. It was a turning point in the process of making decisions, planning the future, and most important, moving forward in peace. It gave resolution to the most painful and recent unchangeable past. Going to the "power spot" that fog-filled morning was an experience for each of the seven women that opened their hearts to view life from the perspective of sorrow from the past, emotional pain, and especially the profound sadness embedded in their soul. That day would change the ritual of expressing in journals hidden secrets to now openly sharing on paper and the empty pages of records yet to come.

My cousins, once or twice, inquired of me about writing the experience down and sent what they had experienced via emails and letters before the year was over. They requested that I write about that morning several times years later because they, too, felt that for the first time the valley beneath the sunrise was filled with waves of fog and wondered if it was somehow connected to my "first time" to join the group. Perhaps the fog could have been in honor of my dad's death? The very reason for my being there for the first time. I remained in silence with any correspondents and conceivably accepted for the first time that sorrow can play off key in a person's mental space. My mind wouldn't let me think in any capacity and I didn't want to.

I wasn't ready to take such a deep dive so soon after my personal loss. Also, there was the distance and time of living so far away that dampened the desire to support others. Being able to say goodbye to beloved members of my family and other hometown residents made my heart full of regrets and sorrow. I had come to learn that the residue of death leaves a void of time that cannot be recaptured because of the difficulty of acceptance. Time provides a bittersweet difficulty of treasuring a loved one once they have been robbed from us because of death.

The others from the "power spot" dwelled in their own private silence afterwards, they, too, had emailed their emotional feelings and vows never to forget that morning. When I received all six "sunrises" from each of the six women, I quickly noted yet another and more personal connection that we all shared. It was that each wanted freedom from the pangs of sadness that is caused by death and to breathe in the memories of the past without grieving. As women we were filled with hope at the "power spot" to live with the past because in reality it's married to the present and the two systematically produce the future that will become our history. So each of us looked into the sunrise with hope! It was the kind of hope that was taught to us from the descendants of people in our families that prayed for and sang songs of hope all their lives. In my younger life I had learned to seek out the first most authentic, and original history book, the Bible. It references death as mankind's last enemy and notes it's "sting" as something we will have to encounter on this earth as we know it one day. This knowledge has caused many to experience a spiritual disconnect of mental and emotional faculties where there is no hope.

During Homecoming celebration, Saturday morning was the sunrise of note. Saturday night was the most active day of various entertainment. Early Sunday morning after the last dance ended, it was a hope to get two or three hours of sleep, maybe, before those who wanted to rise and ready themselves for Sunday morning service needed to wake up. The one existing and operating church was built right behind the original church that unified the community. However, there was another affliation, the A.M.E church, which closed its doors soon after Pastor Joseph Wilson died. Therefore, The First Baptist Church was where families were able to sustain the lives of people that raised their children with steadfast morals. This is where, for their entire lives, they processed the faith they needed to endure another year under tedious circumstance and challenging discouragement!

What remained of the weekend was eventful and always a reminder that soon the little town that entertained upwards of 400 friends, family, and local residents would quickly dwindle and become a place of peace and quiet… or some might say loneliness. Solemn days lay ahead for the small number of residents that found the endurance to weather the feelings of empty Sunday afternoons. They were void of children's laughter and without the enjoyment of evening chatter. Those that left were consumed with mixed feelings and raced away in haste to avoid the tearful task of saying good-bye to those that were not leaving. Only to watch them say farewell to them with broken hearts. This was yet another ritual after the majority of all the homecoming celebrations. It marked another year had passed. The quiet peaceful late Sunday afternoons with empty streets with an occasional couple out for a curious Sunday afternoon drive would soon settle in to close the weekend.

The years that followed continued the tradition that Angela wanted to share, of visiting the hilltop where peace and love could be obtained for other women, to experience hope for their future despite their past. Other women with stories no different than the seven of us anticipated a chance to learn of the connection between their own sunrises and were told of this one-time experience of "going to the power spot!" And when they read about the novelty of this sunrise viewing, they, too, will be empowered from memories of their own visit. What we shared and gave each other as unselfish women that morning wasn't lost nor forgotten. Perhaps for a short time other women will glean a sense of confidence enough to appreciate and trust each other, if just for a miniscule time in their life to grow when they visit this spot. We each wanted change and gained a sense that the journey ahead would be fortified even if the outcome was unknown. The experience was a gift to treasure, to share, and keep for seven lifetimes.

It was a decade before the memory of that day was shared again. It had become one moment in time that the seven of us never spoke of again collectively and would never forget to treasure in our future. My cousin Johnine, once or twice, asked unexpectedly if I had "put words to paper" as she would say. She was the one out of the seven that was most persistent that I compose and share what we had discovered. It didn't take long before it dawned on me why she thought I should be the one to share our "sunrises." My grief was directly linked to that of her own and was the most prevalent and profound at the time. When my dad had passed away, she had also lost another father-figure in her life as well. He was Uncle Boo, her mother's big brother, and friend. It was a most tender and immediate time of sorrow for the family. My dad was the oldest in our seven generation family unit. Whereas the other women returned back home to their families with a new perspective on life and reason to become better at everything they could be, Johnine, Teresa and I still had much grief to process.

So once the sun begins to set, these shared moments that could only happen once in time captured by seven women entitled, "A Kansas Sunrise," a gift to each of her newfound family and sisters, can be shared in the form of a poem Regina wanted to share. The poem is called, "We Speak Your Names." by Pearl Cleage. It was gleaned from an actual life experience and production called, " Flying West." It was a play centered on five women from Nicodemus. It has definitely made a name in the poetry books because of the content. It is

Regina's offering that bonds her own ancestors and family and for any one of us to enjoy as well. And now the story continues for another five women from Nicodemus, along with two others, welcomed to share the journey. Remember that the journey from the past to our future occurs with every new "sunrise." It is the start of every new beginning for all of us to live our best life appreciating our ability to go forward to the end of each day, after each sunset.

"We Speak your Names"

Because we are free women, born of free women who are born of free women, back as far as time begins, we celebrate your freedom. Because we are wise women, born of wise women who are born of wise women, we celebrate your wisdom. Because we are strong women, born of strong women who are born of strong women, we celebrate your strength. Because we are magical women, born of magical women who are born of magical women, we celebrate your magic. My sisters, we are gathered here to speak your

names. We are here because we are your daughters as surely as if you had conceived us, nurtured us, carried us in your wombs, and then sent us out into the world to make our mark and see what we see and be what we be but better, truer, deeper because of the shining example of your own incandescent lives. We are here to speak your names because we have enough sense to know that we did not spring full blown from the forehead of Zeus or arrive on the scene like Topsy, our sister once removed who somehow just grew. We know that we are walking in footprints made deep by the confident strides of women who parted the air before them like the forces of nature that you are. We are here to speak your names because you taught us that the search is always for the truth, and that when people show us who they are, we should believe them. We are here because you taught us that sister speak can continue to be our native tongue, no matter how many languages we learn as we move about as citizens of the world

and of the ever-evolving universe. We are here to speak your names because of the way you made for us. Because of the prayers you prayed for us.

We are the ones you conjured up, hoping we would have strength enough and discipline enough and talent enough and nerve enough to step into the light when it turned in our direction and just smile awhile. We are the ones you hoped would make you proud because all of our hard work makes all of yours part of something better, truer, deeper. Something that lights the way ahead like a lamp unto our feet, as steady as the unforgettable beat of our collective heart. We speak your names. We speak your names.

By Pearl Cleage

The Dedication

This small collection of writings is dedicated to ALL of the Women of Nicodemus from which I acquired and maintained honest insight and integrity. Such lessons were the kind of wisdom these women raised and nurtured their own children to know. They were lessons of responsibilities consumed by every girl child of every decade and age. This would include my cousin, **Angela O. Bates.** Like all of the women from our hometown, she is a daughter and fourth generation descendant of freed slaves from Kentucky. Without her zeal and love of Nicodemus, Kansas and finding her "power spot," these little treasures of wisdom and personal discoveries revealed by seven women perhaps would not have been shared. She has become a sentinel on paper, will always have our support, be supported in spirit from our ancestors and descendants because of the love and blood that bonds us as a family of people that faced the unknown, seeking freedom to live beyond bondage, then and now. These determined and freed black pioneers bookmarked a place in history and courageously made contributions then and now. They lived in this world with the desires of hope and longevity in a peaceful future for all of those that followed. So, in essence, this is for us all, then and now! To my outstanding family and Nicodemus, with much admiration and terms of endearment, we will remain unified! From one corner stone to another, thank you!

A personal thanks to ALL the women that shared a moment in time in their truth!

"Take time to be kind to your truth, it's a door to your heart's freedom!" E.M.Rupp

September 2021

Angela Bates

Johnine Powell

Teresa Switzer

Priscilla (PJ) Bates

Joyce Wilson

Regina Thomas

Earlice "Leesa" Switzer-Rupp

"The Date of Photo: 2015"

"The Lapel Pin of Peace" - 2006

"Summer - July 2018"